JOHN FARMAN

The Very Bloody History of Britain

WITHOUT THE BORING BITS!

PICCADILLY PRESS · LONDON

To Cleo, Polly and Joe

Text and illustrations copyright © John Farman, 1990

Designed by COOPER·WILSON
Phototypeset by Goodfellow & Egan, Cambridge CB4
Printed and bound by Biddles Ltd., Guildford GU1
for the publishers Piccadilly Press Ltd.,
5 Castle Road, London NW1 8PR

British Library Cataloguing in Publication Data
Farman, John
The Very Bloody History of Britain
I. Title
306.708531
ISBN 1-85340-097-1

John Farman is British and lives in South West London. He has
an MA (Design) from the Royal College of Art, and a certificate for
jumping three feet six inches, from Longfield Primary School. He has
worked extensively both in advertising and publishing. Although he
has written and illustrated many books this is his first one for Piccadilly Press.

With special thanks to Dr John Fines and Martin Pannit.

Second impression, 1991
Third impression, 1991

Contents

Introduction

My old teacher 'Basher' Bowker was largely responsible for a disinterest in history that had served me well, right through into adulthood. His dreary lessons seemed, in retrospect, to be an interrogation the like of which hasn't been seen since the Spanish Inquisition. His presentation was so desperately dull, that all I seemed to have been left with was an unparalleled knowledge of paper-dart making and the refined craft of desk-top carving. He used dates as a hunter uses traps. One false move – and the evening would be spent copying out, in my neatest joined-up writing, a mindless repetition of what he said I should have written earlier.

By the time I took my O-level (which I failed magnificently) I could only recite, parrot-fashion, everything one wasn't ever going to be asked about the Industrial Revolution (see boring revolutions) in the eighteenth century, or the Corn Laws of the nineteenth: nothing else! It was a bit like owning a rather dreary jigsaw made drearier by having over half the bits missing, or a bike with no pedals.

Before setting out on this mighty work I knew considerably less British history than the average man in the street (and we all know how thick he is). The further I got

into it, however, the more I realised just what I'd been missing. Our ancestors turn out to be the most fascinating, bloodthirsty, disreputable bunch that you would ever be lucky enough to come across.

Everything you are about to read I've either been told by experts, or read in other books. As everyone's view of history is different, I've steered right down the middle. As it is my book I've chosen the best stories.

I'd like this account of history to be enjoyed. If by some fluke you manage to learn something, don't blame me!

Chapter 1:

Where Do I Come From?

No two people agree about where the first people to live in Britain came from. Mr Patel down the road, was fairly sure they came from India (well he would, wouldn't he), while my chum Seamus Murphy seems to remember being told in the Goat and Shamrock that they came from County Wexford. Although it's common knowledge you could once walk to France, there is no record of England ever being

joined to Ireland. Most confident of all was my old schoolmate Winston who '*knows* they came from Africa'. After asking real experts I've found out Winston's probably right, but I'd never hear the end of it if I told him. Since we now all appear to be immigrants there's probably no such thing as a proper Englishman.

Native Britons
Anyway, wherever we came from, our ancestors were a pretty scruffy, lazy lot spending most of their time hanging around waiting

for history to begin. They only ate what stumbled right in front of them and, unlike their posh relatives in the south of France and Spain, didn't even get round to trying to cheer up their caves by painting those daft-looking animals on their walls. Mind you, there are some amongst us, mentioning no names, who believe they did the caves a favour!

However, when really at a loose end, they did do strange things with huge stones; stacking them in circles or lines like those at Stonehenge or Avebury, probably for no better reason than to drive everyone crazy centuries later trying to work out why they did it.

Long after you couldn't even paddle to France, but long before the Channel was chock-full of strange greasy people swimming backwards and forwards for no apparent reason, the first tourists started turning up. These swarthy continentals didn't have to go through Customs. No ships, no ports — therefore no Customs. They didn't even have to state how long they intended staying. All they had to do was slay anyone who challenged them and set up home wherever they pleased.

This began in 4000 years BC, give or take a century. In those days they always said BC after the date. 'B' stood for 'before' and 'C' stood for 'Christ'. God knows how they knew he was coming.

Simply the fact that they turned up in boats of some kind proves that the new visitors had more marbles than the poor old native Britons, which wasn't difficult. They proceeded to invent clothes, wheels, refrigerators (only joking) and very sharp iron spears which made stabbing our poor forefathers (and foremothers) much quicker and easier.

Meanwhile (and these dates always seem to cause fights among historians)

1,400,000 BC – An unknown apeman lit the first fire.

500,000 BC – First 'upright' man made a sort of tool out of a bit of flint.

25,000 BC – Someone dropped a bit of meat in the fire and discovered it tasted better.

20,000 BC – Wheel invented but proved pretty useless until someone invented another one.

10,000 BC – Weapons used for killing animals and each other.

8600 BC – Someone planted a seed and discovered he could eat what it grew into.

8400 BC – First domesticated dog in North America. Sorry, I don't know his name.

5000 BC – Sea filled up between Britain and Europe (hooray).

2500 BC – Skis invented in Norway. No package holidays till much later however.

1500 BC – Bronze Age hit Britain.

1400 BC – Pharaoh Amenophis got his first engineer to build a water clock. Shadow clocks had been OK, but weren't much use if you'd wanted to check if it was bedtime.

600 BC – Welshman invented the first proper boat – a coracle. It was made from skin stretched over a wooden frame. Amazingly, they've only just stopped using them!

Chapter 2:

The Cunning Celts

Once the new visitors began to settle in, life went quite smoothly until England was invaded properly for the first time by the Celts. They came here in 650 BC from central Europe apparently looking for tin – please don't ask me why! The Celts were tall, blond and blue-eyed and so got all the best girls right away. This, of course, annoyed the poor Britons even more, but there was not much they

could do about it as they only had sticks and fists to fight with. The Celts set up home in the south of England around Surrey and Kent – the stockbroker belt – building flash wooden forts which the poor boneheaded locals could only mill around in awe and envy.

Now England wasn't too bad a place to live for the next few hundred years (providing you were tall, blue-eyed and blond). Then in 55 BC the late great Julius Caesar – star of stage and screen – arrived with a couple of legions from Rome, Italy. The refined Romans were repelled, in more ways than one by the crude Celts, who by this time had turned blue (from woad). They did, however, come back a year later with a much bigger, better-equipped army – and guess what – were repelled again.

55 BC – The Romans

You couldn't get away from the fact, however, that the Romans were much sharper than the Celts – hence the term 'a Roman knows'. They therefore decided that they'd infiltrate peacefully rather than invade; which was just a sneaky Italian trick. How the Celts didn't notice the daftly-dressed Roman soldiers I'll never know.

The first ruler of southern England was a chap called Rex. Under his rule, these smart Italians made money by turning the poor natives into slaves and swapping them for eastern luxuries – probably cheap scent and Turkish Delight.

AD 43 Boadicea

This gradual infiltration took longer than expected and the Romans became rather impatient. Emperor Claudius (of 'I' fame) sent another lot of legions to conquer us properly – which they did – properly! The only real trouble they encountered was a strange woman warrior from somewhere near Norwich. Her name was Boadicea and, from the only available picture I've seen, she seemed to travel everywhere in a very snazzy horse-drawn cart with blades sticking out of the wheels. This must have made parking in London rather tricky, which is probably why she burnt it to the ground. She went on to kill 70,000 Romans but, when they started getting the better of things, poisoned herself. (Some people are such bad losers!)

SPOT THE ROMAN!

Chapter 3:

When In Britain Do As the Romans Do

If you can't beat a Roman, join him. Gradually the hostile Brits came round to the Roman way of thinking. The smart ones even managed to make a few lire and live Hollywood-style, in centrally heated villas covered in naff mosaics. The unsmart ones stayed in their hovels, being only serfs and slaves. Let's face it, we can't all be chiefs or there'd be no Indians! Soon everybody knew their place. Christianity was made the imperial religion and the first two centuries (whew! AD at last) were to be among the most prosperous and peaceful in England's history.

The Scottish Highlands were a no-go area because the Picts and the Scots were far too rough and beastly. The Romans, who only knew how to build dead-straight roads, soon gave up on mountainous Wales. Mind you, I expect they soon changed their tune when they discovered gold in the hills.

Furthermore, they ignored Devon and Cornwall not only because they were terribly barren and remote, but also because beaches and cream teas hadn't been invented yet.

They therefore stuck to ruling England. Hadrian, the new Supremo in Rome, decided around AD 130 to build a socking great wall, once described as 'the rampart of sods', right across the north of England. The theory behind it was obvious. If those ghastly Picts and Scots wouldn't let 'em in, then the Romans wouldn't let 'em out!

AD 350 – Mini-Romes
So for the next couple of centuries all the new 'associate citizens' of the Roman Empire had a fairly grief-free time. Anyone who was anyone, except the serfs and slaves, intermarried and started talking Latin. Mini-Romes like Bath (hence bath) and Verulamium (hence St Albans) became dead-posh centres of culture and high life. Best of all, there wasn't some hairy yobbo hammering on your door threatening to rape and pillage you every five minutes.

Back in Rome, it seems that life had become one continuous party. When they weren't having orgies (which sound rather fun), or making movies like 'Ben Hur' or 'Spartacus', they'd idle away their hours converting Christians – to lion food. Unfortunately, they were having such a brilliant time that they carelessly neglected the rest of their Empire, which soon started to decline and fall. I wonder if that would make a title for a book?

Meanwhile

55 BC – Romans brought heated bathrooms, glass windows, swimming pools, temples, aqueducts, proper writing, chariot races, kids' dolls and good wine.

4 BC – Christ is born. I know! You don't have to tell me. How can he have been born four years before himself? Apparently an almighty cock-up was made in the sixth century when calculating the calendar and it was too late to do anything about it.

Chapter 4:

A Horrible Hole In Hadrian's Wall

Build a wall and before long everyone will want to be on the other side of it (see East Berlin). The Picts and the Scots were no exception. In AD 367, when the Romans were at their wits' end

EARLY SCOTTISH DOG

trying to keep the horrid hordes at bay, the McScoundrels broke through and were extremely unpleasant to everyone they ran into.

AD 400 – Angles, Saxons and Jutes

If, at the time, you managed to escape with your life (and your wife) from the Picts and Scots, you could bet your last goat you'd meet a bunch of Saxon pirates coming the other way. They'd just waded ashore with their mates, the Angles and Jutes, from Denmark and Germany. What is it with those Germans? If you thought the Scots were uncouth this crowd had no couth whatsoever. They were tearing up and down the Roman roads ravaging and ravishing everything that hadn't been ravaged and ravished by the first lot! The Romans, fed up with horde-hindering, packed their bags and high-tailed it back to Rome in AD 407.

The poor old Celts, who'd become somewhat refined (Roman style), could hardly believe what was happening. Many had turned to Christianity, which was all the rage after the Roman Emperor Constantine had given it the thumbs up. Seeing that there was no point hanging around, they packed up and rushed off to Wales and the Cornish peninsula where they all opened tea 'shoppes'. So

YE NEW TEA SHOPPE

ROMAN STYLE CLOTHES

you have this incredible scenario: one minute all the nice guys are in the middle surrounded by hooligans, and then, before you can say King Arthur, it's all about face. The remaining heathen peasants never took baths or went in for culture. All they did manage to keep from the Roman occupation were the roads and the pheasants (another Roman first).

AD 500 – The Irish

Believe it or not, the Irish, at this time, were the good boys of Britain – having not invented Guinness yet. Being mostly monks and saints they appeared to spend all their time praying and illuminating manuscripts (what went wrong?).

THE FIRST BAD IRISH THOUGHT.

AD 500 – King Arthur

When King Arthur was invented, as he well might have been, in the beginning of the fifth century, he became the champion of all those Christians who'd run away. He was an odd king, by all accounts, spending most of his time chatting round round tables, with his tinned cronies (see armour). He had a magic sword called Excalibur which, having spent ages trying to pull from a rock, he proceeded to chuck into a lake. He was never able to be away on bat-tle business for long because his wife, Guinevere, who appar-ently was a great looker, spent too much time at night with knights. Hence the famous line – 'Once a knight is enough'.

HAVE YOU MISSED ME DEAREST?

AD 520 – More Royals

Even the Saxons eventually ran out of people to fight with and the natives, having forgotten Rome and Christianity, were quite happy to settle down to peace and quiet as if nothing had ever happened (history please note!). They did have a big thing about kings, however, and divided England up into seven – yes, seven – kingdoms. These were Kent, Sussex, Essex, Wessex (south), Northumbria, East Anglia and Mercia (midlands). Imagine having seven Royal families to support!

Meanwhile

AD 407 – The Romans took all the great stuff in the last 'Meanwhile' back home to Italy.

Chapter 5:

Here Come The Vikings

In AD 597 a monk called Mr Augustine (he wasn't a saint yet) was sent by Pope Gregory to convert these nice new Anglo Saxons to Christianity again. With a little help from his 'monky' friends it took just half a century. This brought us into a sort of ecclesiastical common market with Europe and everybody got educated again. Hallelujah!

England settled down and there followed a couple of boring centuries during which farming was in, and fighting was out. Egbert of Wessex became head king and everything seemed jolly peaceful until . . .

Vikings and Danes

Towards the middle of the eighth century, what had been the odd raid at the seaside, turned into a full-blown invasion by the dreaded Vikings and Danes. These guys were even taller, blonder and

tougher than the last lot. They came in huge pointy boats with dragons' heads on the fronts (sorry prows), wearing daft tin hats with horns on. They managed to make mincemeat of the natives who'd forgotten how to fight. The Vikings from Norway started in the north of Scotland and worked down; while the Danes from Denmark hit the east and went west.

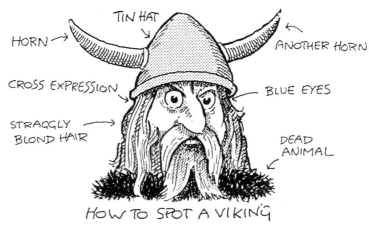

AD 870 – Alfred

The Danes were eventually stopped by the great Alfred the Great who was then King of Wessex. He persuaded them to stay where they were, letting them have all the towns ending in 'by' – ie Rugby and Derby. The rest jumped back in their boats and shot over to northern France, calling the bit where they stopped, Normandy. Our Alfred was a great scholar and taught his people to speak like this:

Swa claene hio waes oðfaellenu on Andlekynne ðaette swþiðe feawe waeron behionan Humbre þe hiora ðenunga cuðan understandan on Englisc.

This means 'So clean was it fallen away in England that very few were there on this side of the Humber who could understand their service books in English'.

They didn't really learn to talk properly (like what we do), for another three hundred years or so.

AD 975 – Conquered Again

Alfred died in 900 leaving a fairly peaceful land (and a few dodgy cakes). This quiet life was only to be mucked up by King Ethelred the Unready some years later when he foolishly massacred a whole load of Danes which really annoyed them. This brought about another invasion in 1016 by a very cross Sweyn Forkbeard who captured England and sent Ethelred – who still wasn't ready – packing. His son, Canute, became King of England and big white chief of the whole Scandinavian Empire. When poor Ethelred died,

23

Canute really got his rather damp feet under the table by marrying Ethelred's widow, who was obviously no fool. His feet became damp (and he became legendary) following an incident on the beach one day. His grovelling courtiers reckoned their boss would only have to say the word and the tide would stop advancing. Canute, rather sceptically, tried it but got drenched. He was, by all accounts, a bit grumpy and prone to severe barbarity and crime. Gradually, however, it seems he cheered up and became rather nice and even a bit popular.

1041 – Edward
Unfortunately this particular Empire collapsed shortly after, so Ethelred's boy, Edward the Confessor, got England back which was a real stroke of luck. I must confess, however, that Edward was a bit of a wimp, so all the real ruling was done by Harold, Earl of Wessex, who was head of the anti-Norman party (poor Norman!). When Harold was made king it really annoyed Edward's French cousin, Monsieur William Conqueror (head Norman), who decided to get an army together to invade England yet again.

By the Way
The Vikings managed to work themselves into such a fury (now thought to be drug induced) that they roared, howled, slashed, and even bit anything in their path. The people who managed to escape from these invincible furry madmen, described them as 'berserk' which in Norse-talk means 'clad in bearskin'.

Meanwhile
  AD 500 – Stirrups invented, taking pressure off certain parts of the anatomy.
  AD 550 – St David converted the wicked Welsh to Christianity.
  AD 563 – St Columba did the same for the Picts.
  AD 890 – Horseshoes invented (four), to stop horses wearing their legs down to their knees.
  AD 891 – Alfred the Great started writing a history of England. It's not fair, he only had a few centuries to swot up!

AD 950 – Padded horsecollars saved a lot of horses (and probably a few serfs) from choking to death when pulling heavy loads.

AD 1000 – Everybody thought that the day of judgement was due and that the world was going to end. Bet they felt stupid in 1001!

Chapter 6:

Halfway House

1066 was probably the most important date in history. Harold, England's heroic King (how can you have a hero called Harold?), was at his London home confidently awaiting a call summoning him to repel cousin Will (the Norman) who was expected

SORRY! NOT INVENTED YET

any day. Unfortunately, Harold was called away at the last minute on more pressing invasion business up north. It was those blessed Norwegians again. Just as he got there, and had shooed them off, he got the message that William was bringing his greedy garçons ashore on the south coast. If it had been nowadays he could have hopped in his Limo, belted down the M1 and been there before they could say 'allo allo'. Rushing back southwards, however, he could only round up 7,000 men who, by the time they arrived, were so knackered that they were carved up mercilessly. Poor Harold got something in his eye for his trouble and it was probably an arrow. Anyway it was enough to kill him, so unfortunately it's, 'Bye-bye, Harold'.

1087 – William the Conqueror

So it was another fine mess the Brits had gotten themselves into. The Normans had little trouble sorting out anyone who got in their way, including Hereward the Wake, possibly the son of Lady Godiva (famous nude mother), who was soon put back to sleep. William was crowned and suddenly everyone was French.

NUDE MUM

NUDE HORSE

All this features in the very first embroidered cartoon strip called the Bayeux Tapestry which was very long and very, very unfunny. Will's first major headache was how to sort out what he'd just conquered. He commissioned this whacking great book, known as the DOMESDAY BOOK which listed everyone in the country, rich and poor, and everything they owned down to the last chicken (and egg). This was to prove a real boon when working out how much tax he could sting everyone for. Lawyers and civil servants hadn't been discovered (along with many other useless inventions).

The Feudal System

William created the feudal system which was, almost, very clever. The deal was that the king snatched all the property from the Anglo-Saxon earls, and divvied it up amongst his barons who were called tenants-in-chief. In return for this they would drum him up

an army. They in turn sub-let their land to the Norman knights, called sub-tenants, who would do the actual fighting (those barons weren't daft). Under them were the poor old Saxon serfs and villeins. These poor so-and-so's were given measly strips of land, about the size of your average back garden, which they were allowed to farm for about ten minutes a week. They, of course, had to give rent, food, their pretty daughters and the rest of their time, farming the boss's land. AND they were supposed to tug their forelocks in gratitude. If anyone objected, William had a neat solution. He sent a bunch of his merry men round to burn down the village and kill all the animals. Problem solved!

Law and Order

The tenants-in-chief had their own courts as there was very little common law in the country. The king was represented by a sheriff (usually from Nottingham) who was in charge of every shire. Even so, there were quite a lot of outlaws and hoods (see Robin) who robbed the poor to pay the rich. Is that right?

What this meant, when you got down to the nitty gritty, was that all rank and power depended on what you owned. Some things never change! On the other hand it could be said that William now owned the whole shooting match and had rented England out.

By 1135 the English knew their place and were just beginning to speak Le Francais bon. Most people now reckon that the Norman Conquest wasn't such a bad thing, otherwise we could well be Scandinavian by now – driving around in Volvos, eating open sandwiches and beating ourselves with twigs (no thanks!). Anyway the now-nice Normans built lots of brill churches and castles and gradually the country began to run OK again.

By the Way

William has been recorded as one of the strongest men in history being able to jump on his horse wearing full armour. I notice his poor old horse doesn't get a mention.

Here's another little story. William died in 1087 when his horse threw him: the stupid steed trod on a hot ember from a town his master had just razed (or lowered) to the ground. Old William was so fat that when they tried to squeeze him into his sarcophagus (a stone coffin) it burst open and so did he! The smell was so horrid that everyone fled the church in Caen, Franch (urggh). In 1562 vandals broke into his magnificent tomb and stole all of him except a thigh bone which was given another burial eighty years later. Even that got nicked by looters during the French Revolution, so his tomb now stands empty. Nobody seems to know what happened to the horse.

Chapter 7:

Brotherly Love! – 1087

When William died, his son Rufus – who was really William II – took over England while his elder son Robert, got Normandy. Rufus was so named because when he blew his top – which was often – he'd go bright red. Rufus was apparently a bit of a naughty boy. He grew his hair long, got drunk, went out with boys, and generally found being king much more fun than anyone previously. He reigned for thirteen years, always under threat from his jealous brother. It was just as Robert was about to attack in 1100, spurred on by his rich, bossy wife, that Rufus fell off his horse (with an arrow in his back) while hunting and died. It obviously ran

in the family. Most people felt the 'accident' was a judgement from God and so weren't the least bit surprised when the tower of Winchester Cathedral collapsed on his tomb a year later.

1100 – Henry I

Suspiciously, Rufus's younger brother, Henry, happened to be in the forest the day he died. You don't have to be very bright to put two and two together and conclude that he might have had something to do with it. Henry I, therefore, inherited the throne, a big sparkly hat and a brand new enemy. When Robert did attack, Henry managed to smooth-talk his way out of it and gave his brother a pension of £2000 a year to stay away. Then Henry had  second thoughts, and, being a crafty beggar, kept giving his brother a hard time. He eventually nobbled brother Bob and deposited him in his dingy dungeons for twenty-eight years until he died, aged eighty. (Charming!)

Chapter 8:

Chaos! – 1135

This bit of history goes crazy.

Henry I was king for thirty years and married to a Matilda, as was his father. When he died in 1135, from an over indulgence in lampreys (little eels), he left only one legitimate heir (and twenty who weren't!). Her name was also Matilda and, although only recently a widow, her dad made her marry fourteen-year-old Geoffrey Plantagenet Fulk (what a mouthful) of Anjou. The deal was that, when she eventually became queen, it would expand the family empire.

Henry's nephew, Stephen, had other ideas and told a huge fib. He informed everyone that Uncle Henry had told him, on his deathbed, that he wanted Stephen to be king. When safely under the crown, just to confuse everybody, he married another Matilda. Perhaps the name Matilda was the twelfth century equivalent of Tracey. Anyway, there was a huge argument, followed by a civil war in which everyone pinched each other's castles and Matildas.

1135 – Civil War

Geoffrey died, and his son Henry – another one – took over the fight (confused yet?). He – that's still the other one – then married Eleanor of Aquitaine, the ex-wife of Louis VII of France, who was so cross he joined forces with Stephen. If anyone's still keeping up with this, please let me know!

To cut a long story short, Henry and Stephen did a deal. In 1153, at the Treaty of Westminster, it was agreed that Stephen should stay king for the rest of his life and then Henry could have a go which sounded rather fair if you ask me. This turned out to be brilliant for Henry, because Stephen keeled over a year later. None of the Matildas were ever heard of again until centuries later in Australia, of all places, where one was believed to have invented the waltz!

1154 – Henry II

So Henry II copped the lot. All of England and most of the left hand bit of France. Best of all, nobody wanted to fight him for it. The first thing he did was to demolish all Stephen's unlicenced castles. Hands up who knows what a castle licence looks like? Then, instead of using the feudal nobility (the barons) to keep down the English, as William the Conqueror had done, he used the English to keep down the feudal nobility (neat eh!). He then got rid

of all the sheriffs and set up a proper legal system with judges and juries. This replaced trial by combat. Shame, really – I always thought it sounded rather a laugh (and quicker!). In fact, the whole system of trial and punishment at this time is worthy of a closer look.

Crime and Punishment

One of the best ways of finding out whether a chap was guilty of a crime, was to try him by fire. The accused was made to carry a

piece of red-hot iron for three paces whereupon his hand was bound up (nice of them!). If, when it was undone three days later, there were no blisters, he was innocent, but if he had blisters he was punished and even killed. It might have been a smart idea to put the bandage on the other hand.

Cheats and thieves were put in the stocks, which allowed all the villagers to laugh and throw rotten food at them. (Football hooligans? I wonder.) Furthermore, bakers who sold stale bread were carted around the town on a sledge with loaves tied to their necks, while fishmongers who sold bad goods would have rotting fish tied round theirs. I think a word to our local trading standards officers might give them some new ideas.

Bad priests would have to ride through the town facing their horse's backside wearing a paper crown (the priest – silly) and, even better, nagging wives would be fitted with a Scold's Bridle, which had a piece of metal to hold their wagging tongues down. I wonder if they had one for door-to-door salesmen?

Ears and hands were lopped off and noses slit at the drop of a hat, but torture for fun, as such, was forbidden.

Henry II was also to become (in)famous for invading Ireland and martyring his archbishop and best friend, Thomas Becket, who'd been throwing his weight around. He was a great and energetic king, however, galloping from one end of his empire to the other, appearing to be everywhere at once. Apart from having a few rebellious sons, everything went like clockwork (yet to be invented) until his demise in 1189.

By the Way

Poor Thomas wasn't to rest easy in his grave. 350 years after his death that naughty old Henry VIII (see Henry VIII), determined to have yet another go at him, had him dug up. The poor old saint's skeleton was brought before England's Star Chamber and accused of 'usurping papal authority'. After a formal trial, which must have looked a touch weird, his bones – strangely unable to defend themselves – were convicted of high treason and publicly burned. Things never seem to go right for some people.

JUST ANSWER THE QUESTION

Chapter 9:

Nice Richard And Horrible John

The first son, Richard the Lionheart, was handsome, kind, brave, clever, romantic, popular, and King of England and a big bit of France.

The second son, John, was ugly, cruel, cowardly, clever (also), unromantic, unpopular and only got Ireland.

The other two brothers carelessly died!

1189 – Richard the Lionheart

Strangely enough England liked Richard, but Richard didn't seem to like England. He preferred to spend all his time on his Christian Crusade (basically attacking when you think you're in the right) against the mighty Saladin who was head of the Muslims – otherwise known as infidels – in the Holy Land. It was while he was away that he got a call telling him that brother John was revolting. He got the first ship home, but was shipwrecked near Aquileia and had to walk the rest of the way. While strolling gaily (which some say he was) through Germany he was arrested and thrown into gaol. The greedy Krauts asked the English for £3,000,000 to get him back. While his fans were trying to raise the cash he was kept in a secret place. After a year his favourite minstrel Blondel – 'how

34

favourite?' I hear you ask – toured Europe strumming the boss's favourite tune outside every castle. The Germans must have thought he was barmy. One day Richard joined in the chorus and was found. He eventually came home, sorted out his bad brother and then, barely having time to unpack, rushed back to La Belle France to try to win back some of the lands lost while in prison. He didn't do badly apart from being killed in 1199. It was a bolt from a crossbow, which curiously enough he'd introduced into France, that finished him. There's gratitude for you! The path was now clear for the dreadful John.

1199 – King John

Now John really was someone you wouldn't let marry your daughter. A really nasty piece of work, grabbing cash from all his poor downtrodden subjects so that he could live in luxury and defend his French possessions. Come to think of it, I thought that was what Royalty was all about. He was always bad at battles (they didn't call him 'Softsword' for nothing) and lost most of them. He murdered Arthur his young nephew in 1203 because he had a better claim to the throne, and got into such trouble that, in the war that followed, he lost nearly all of what remained of his French dominions. He was always watching his back, as he was convinced all his men were trying to kill him. You can't really blame him, however, because they were!

His favourite hobby was extorting money from his subjects, which hacked off the public more than anything else. Then, just to put the tin lid on it, he upset the Church and was excommunicated (not allowed to talk to God). This didn't worry John too much – not being much of a churchgoer – but he did, out of spite, grab all the Church's possessions.

A bunch of barons, fed up with the fine mess John was getting the country into, rebelled and captured London (can you imagine?) and made him stick his seal on the Magna Carta in 1215. This famous document not only pointed out what a cock-up he and his ancestors had made of ruling, but also greatly reduced his enormous power. Sealing was one thing, but as he was a fully paid up creep, getting him to change his ways was a different matter.

In the end the rebels invited Prince Louis of France to come and sit on our throne (what cheek!), which he tried for five minutes in 1216. A long civil war followed, but John died that very year.

By the Way
John's enemies nearly killed themselves laughing when:

1. John had to watch most of his baggage train, with all his precious jewels, disappear under quicksands in the Wash. This

certainly disproves the old saying – everything comes out in the wash!

2. King John, famous for his disgusting feeding habits, literally ate himself to death in 1216.

Meanwhile
1100 – Knives and forks were brought back from the Crusades (who says Saladin's lot were barbarians?).
1120 – The Chinese invented playing cards.
1130 – Court of the Exchequer formed. A huge checked tablecloth was laid out, and coins were placed in the squares to help the court count incoming revenue.

1140 – Spices and pepper used in Britain for the first time.

1180 – Glass windows were used instead of brick ones! I bet that improved the view.

1180 – First windmills seen in Europe.

1185 – Oxford University began.

1209 – Just like the Boat Race – Cambridge came second.

1214 – Bacon invented – Roger Bacon. He was a great scientist, predicting automobiles, ocean liners and aeroplanes; so clever, in fact, that his monk mates called him a heretic and eventually threw him into jail.

Chapter 10:

Hooray For Henry – 1216

John's nine-year-old son, Henry III, was to turn out better at battles than his dad. When he was crowned he left virtually all the country-running to a council (which grew up into the first Parliament). When he came of age he started throwing his weight around and upset everyone by giving all the best jobs to his wife Eleanor's foreign relatives.

He got even more stick when he gave his son Edmund the island of Sicily. Lucky little beggar, the most I ever got was a train set! Henry had just been given it by the Pope. The snag was that the Pope had 'forgotten' to tell Henry that Emperor Frederick's son, Manfred, was actually living there, and that he'd have to conquer it. This turned out to be a touch expensive (conquering usually is) and a daft thing to do. Eventually, Parliament said enough's enough and took the government out of Henry's hands.

This caused a bit of a civil war in which a chap called Simon de Montfort, who was quite a rebel, managed to take over the country. He came to a sticky end when Henry's other boy, Edward, defeated and dismembered him at the Battle of Evesham (a very bad way of losing your arms and legs).

1272 – Edward Plantagenet
Edward became King (and the I) in 1272. He was very aggressive but strangely popular with the general public. With their help he checked the power of the barons and Parliament. The Church was also getting a trifle big for its ecclesiastical boots. A terrible nationalism – thinking your country's the best – swept through this green and pleasant land, resulting in most of the foreigners and all of the Jews being kicked out (sound familiar?).

Edward then turned on the Welsh who had always been a bit stroppy. He hunted down Llewelyn, the head Celt, killed him and left loads of soldier-filled castles to keep them quiet. Llewelyn has since become a cult hero with today's Welsh nationalists.

1305 – The Scots
He tried the same thing with Scotland, and managed to hang, draw, and quarter their leader William Wallace – a good way of being in four places at the same time. He also stole their Stone of Scone (or

was it Scone of Stone?) on which all their kings had been crowned. Keep it quiet, but if you peek under the throne in Westminster Abbey tomorrow, you'll see the English have still got it (tee hee!). Anyway, in spite of all this, he couldn't quite beat them and, in the end, Robert the Bruce, their best ever fighter, was made King of Scotland.

Robert looked round for allies and soon became best chums with France. Can you imagine a Scotsman with a French accent? (Mon McDieu!) In 1307 Edward died, aged sixty-eight, at Carlisle, still trying to catch Bruce the Robert who kept running away and hiding.

During his reign Edward managed to upset the 'Model Parliament' by continually jacking up the wool tax – so fleecing the farmers – to pay for all his battles with the French and the Scots. Parliament cleverly tacked a bit on the Magna Carta which basically said that he had to ask them first if he wanted to do anything (spoilsports!).

Apart from little squabbles like this, however, the thirteenth (1200–1300) had been a jolly good century – much more fun than in Norman times.

Meanwhile

1233 – Coal mined in England.

1250 – Goose quills discovered to be
good for writing (and quite good for geese).

1250 – Westminster Abbey, thought to be
out of date, pulled down and rebuilt in Early English style.

1250s – English spoken as a main language.

Sumer is icumen in
Lhude sing cuccu!
Groweth sed, and bloweth med,
And springeth the wude nu –
Sing cuccu!

Well! It's almost English.

1290 – Spectacles invented.

1290 – Mechanical clock invented, but no one seems to know by whom.

Chapter 11:

Out Out Damn Scot!

Edward I's son called 'II' was a bit of a good-for-nothing I'm afraid. He spent most of his time squandering the poor's hard-earned cash with his two best chums (also good-for-nothings) Piers Gaveston and Hugh Despenser – I wonder what he dispensed? When his father died, England's relations with Wales, Ireland, Scotland and France couldn't have been worse. Unfortunately, young 'II' was behind the door when tact was handed out, and all he managed to do was make things worse still. On top of all this the English barons were getting nastier and nastier. They murdered poor Piers, dispensed with Hugh and grabbed the government. If this wasn't enough Robert the Bruce the Robert, bored with being attacked, started raiding the north of England. He even managed to personally give Henry de Bohn (our top knight), a neat centre parting with his axe at the battle of Bannockburn in 1314.

1322 – Edward Beats the Barons

Honestly, it really was no fun being king in those days. Any plan poor Edward had for Britain to be one big happy family went right down the pan, and he was becoming extremely grumpy. Suddenly he snapped, and, after a short sharp battle with the barons, took all the power back. There was no peace for poor Eddie, however, as the next year things got even worse!

Finally in 1327 everyone possible had a go at him, forcing him to abdicate – which means give up being king (most people would have been quite glad).

If that wasn't bad enough his wife (the queen) and her boyfriend backed by a bunch of bad barons imprisoned Edward in a disused well and then did him in! It never reigns but it pours!!!

41

1327 – Edward III

Time for another Edward again. This time the unlucky fellow was only fifteen, and became a father and the III in the same year (more fool him). Like his old man, he was really good at spending the country's hard-earned cash fighting anyone and everyone. Another irritating habit was his slaughtering of any subjects who complained, which they didn't like one bit. He did, however, run one of the poshest courts ever, with all his friends and relatives dressed up in hitherto unseen finery (a bit like in 'Come Dancing' – urgh). Tournaments, jousting and feasting were all the rage and the court's revels were the gossip of home and abroad.

But history also has a nasty habit of repeating itself, and soon his friends became restless and started plotting against him – a national pastime.

1337 – 100 Years War

Edward's main claim to fame, however, was starting the biggest and best war ever, which went on for a hundred years and was called, (surprisingly), the Hundred Years War. Again, how did they know it would last that long? Three guesses who it was against? You're right – our old mates, the French. Strangely enough it was popular with nearly everyone – except those who never came back – and Parliament even gave Edward tons of money to spend on ships, soldiers and swords, etc. The trouble was, it was only a loan and they soon wanted it back. Poor Edward, as always, was flat broke, so paying back the odd million quid was out of the question. He was, therefore, the first king (and last) to go bankrupt.

The first twenty years of the war went splendidly and our brave lads, led by the King and his son, the Black Prince (so called

42

because of his groovy black armour), went through the French like a knife through butter – or should I say beurre. At the Battle of Crécy the score was England 15,000, France 100. Unfortunately, while they were all away having a 'bon' time killing the Frogs (and being killed), something rather unpleasant happened back home. Half the English died!!!!

1348 – The Black Death

It seems impossible. About 2,000,000 of our ancestors snuffed it. They had all caught a fascinating foreign disease from a group of travelling fleas who'd caught it from a group of travelling rats. It was called the Black Death because:

1. It turned you black.
2. It killed you!

This plague is now regarded as just about the most infectious ever known and very few people have ever recovered from it.

Having half the population six feet under was hugely inconvenient. For a start, there was hardly a spare man able to go to France – to get killed, and furthermore there were very few left to cultivate the land. They didn't starve as, fortunately, there was practically no one around to eat anything anyway.

Nevertheless, the few natives that were left were getting restless. The war was costing a bomb and the Church was running riot, with monks and friars doing a load of naughty things that monks and friars weren't supposed to do (use your imagination!). Also there was a heavy traffic in indulgences or pardons. A pardon was a piece of paper that absolved the purchaser from all guilt from his (or her) indiscretions in the eyes of God. They were also a neat way for the Pope – at this time there were two! – to make

pocketfuls of cash. Instead of the normal confession that a Catholic gets free in church today, the crafty old Popes were flogging them throughout the world like raffle tickets.

Meanwhile

1291	– Saladin and the Saracens captured Acre. Final whistle blows at the Crusades.
1314	– The first St Paul's Cathedral finished.
1315,16,20,21	– Terrible harvests caused famine and disease.
1328	– Sawmill invented.

1337 – First weather forecast by William Merlee of Oxford. I bet it was wrong.

1340–1400 – Geoff Chaucer wrote books like *The Canterbury Tales*.

I THINK ITS GOING TO RAIN.

Chapter 12:

The Peasants Are Revolting

By 1377 the picture had changed quite a bit in England. France had captured the Isle of Wight – shock! horror! The Black Prince was dead (from overfighting). His poor old dad, Edward, who'd gone slightly round the bend, was being practically spoon-fed by one Alice Perrers – who sounds far too down-market to be a king's mistress. She was also having the odd spoonful herself having requisitioned all of his dead wife Philippa's priceless jewellery. The Black Prince's brother, John of Gaunt (where's Gaunt?), was virtually running the country and as soon as dukes were invented, he became the Duke of Lancaster – the first of a famous dynasty. (Burt Lancaster?)

By the time poor old loony Edward died, England had lost nearly all of France except Calais. This was no great loss, as in those days you couldn't even nip across the old Channel for a few bottles of the old duty free vino. Strangely enough, historians record Edward as being rather a good king. Mind you, they didn't have to live with him!

1377 – Richard II

Little Richard (II) the Black Prince's ten-year-old lad was the next king. They sound a bit like rock stars don't they? After being crowned, he carried on 'the Expensive War' heavily advised by his uncle John of Lancaster – or was it Duke of Gaunt?

In order to raise funds he charged the first poll tax – but certainly not the last! Every male over sixteen had to pay one shilling (5p). This probably sounds fairly reasonable to you, but if you consider that your average sulky serf earned a penny (½p) a day you'll understand how miffed they all were. It was not unusual for the collectors to be burned alive or have their heads cut off. You might think this a little excessive, but we won't take a vote on it.

1381 – Wat Tyler

Suddenly the erstwhile pleasant peasants were really revolting. They were led by a certain Wat Tyler from Kent. Nobody seems to know what Wat did in Kent, but he brought them all to London anyway where they pillaged and burned everything they came across – a bit like Cup Final night these days. The King promised them everything they asked for, but it seems he had his fingers crossed because when the main crowd had dispersed, the mayor stabbed Wat for his cheek (Wat cheek!) and his friends were all hanged – for theirs!

Richard II married Anne (a REAL Bohemian) but they were to have no children – maybe the fact that he preferred men might have had something to do with it.

Things didn't run smoothly, however, and soon poor Richard was getting real stick from a posh gang called the Lords Appellant led by his cousin Henry and his uncle Gloucester. This suave bunch packed into Parliament one day and forced it to exile or execute all Richard's friends. Richard didn't think this was a terribly nice thing for your family to do, so nine years later, after much planning, he and his mates piled back into Parliament and turned the tables. They murdered his uncle (by suffocation) and exiled his cousin Henry. When John of Gaunt died, Richard snatched all the vast estates that made up the Duchy of Lancaster.

Henry IV

Rather unfairly Richard's supporters thought he'd gone too far and backed John of Gaunt's son Henry (the one in exile), who came back with his own army to get his dead dad's Duchy back. Poor

Richard was then de-throned and chucked into the tower where he was – you've guessed it – murdered. There followed the famous line from Henry on his way to be made king:

'In the name of Fadir Son and Holy Ghost, I Henry of Lancaster chalenge this Rewme of Ingland and the Corone.'

This might be much better English, but it's still a hoot if you say it out loud!

After the crowning ceremony Henry and his friends sat down to the following meal:

FIRST COURSE

Brawn in pepper and spice sauce – Royal pudding – Boar's head – Fat chicken – Herons – Pheasants (not peasants) – Cygnets (small swans) – Date and prune custard (yuk!) – Sturgeon and pike.

SECOND COURSE

Venison in boiled wheat and milk – Jelly – Stuffed sucking pig – Peacocks – Roast bitterns – Glazed chicken – Cranes (birds silly!) – Roast venison – Rabbits – Fruit tarts – Cold brawn – Date pudding.

ANY KETCHUP?

THIRD COURSE

Beef in wine and almond sauce – Preserved quinces – Roast egrets (little herons) – Curlews. Pine nuts in honey and ginger – Partridges – Quails – Snipe – Tiny birds – Rissoles glazed with egg yolks – Rabbits (again!) – Sliced brawn – Iced eggs – Fritters – Cheesecakes – Small rolls.

I bet you'd rather have a Big Mac, large fries and a chocolate shake!

By the Way

The first thing Henry did on being crowned was to have poor Richard embalmed and put on display in full royal kit. He was finally laid to rest in Westminster Abbey where they thoughtfully left a hole in the side of the tomb so that passers-by could touch the ex-king's head. One day, years later in 1776, a naughty schoolboy nicked his jawbone and took it home to his mum and dad (at least he didn't give it to the dog!).

TEACHING AN OLD DOG NEW TRICKS

Chapter 13:

Punch-up With The Percys

Although Henry had become IV in 1399 he wasn't taken that seriously because:
1. He'd got there by force and
2. Wasn't really next in line.
He was, therefore, bossed about by Parliament and, worse, the

Church, (which was keeping warm burning heretics – mostly called Lollards). As usual, there were punch-ups all over the shop; the most serious being that with the Percys from Northumberland, led by Lord Percy who, strange as it may seem, had put Henry on the throne in the first place (fickle? – not half!). The Percys joined up with the stroppy Scots and wild Welsh again but were beaten hollow at Shrewsbury. Percy's son Henry Hotspur – who sounds like a northern comedian – was severely killed.

It appears that Henry IV lived on the back of his horse (sorry, we don't know its name), tearing up and down Olde England fighting everyone. He did make it up with the French, however, and stopped attacking them for a few minutes. England became quite peaceful, and shortly afterwards he died – probably of boredom.

1413 – Henry V

In 1413 his son Hal became Henry V. Now Hal had been a bit of a lad in part I of his life (see Shakespeare), knocking around with some very dodgy ladies and a fat old drunk called Falstaff. When he was 'kinged', however, he got his act together and, having developed quite a taste for that old Lollard burning himself, executed his old mate Falstaff for good measure. When he heard that the King of France had gone barmy he thought it might be quite a giggle to go a-conquering. Watch out you Frogs!

He turned out to be rather good at this and, to cut a long story short (and loads of soldiers), he really knocked the stuffing out of them, particularly at Agincourt. So well, in fact, that he married the daughter of mad Charles VI (known as Charles the Silly) of France and became Regent (nearly king) of all France. Just as all was going well, Henry caught something rather unpleasant at Vincennes and died aged thirty-five. In the same year, the now completely wacko Charles VI of France, suffered the same fate.

By the Way

It might be of interest to note that the English soldiers won principally because of the superiority of the longbow over the crossbow, owing to their ability to reload much faster. Two fingers were used to draw a longbow string back so even without the actual bow the Frogs still got the message. The famous two finger gesture which means 'Please go forth and multiply', can be directly traced to Agincourt.

Chapter 14:

King Of The Cradle – 1422

Henry VI became the first sovereign to wear nappies. At nine months old he became king of both England and France and had to wear two crowns. No problem, you might think. Well yes, it could have been all right had it not been for a rather strange French woman called Joan of Arc (where's Arc?). Now she really

was a fruitcake. She wore men's clothes and heard strange voices telling her to fight the English who she called the 'Goddams' (Goddam whats?).

She turned out to be rather good at war and actually kept the Brits at bay, helping 'hommes' like Dunois – known, rather rudely, as the bastard of Orleans. She was eventually captured by the Burgundians who were on our side. They, rather ungraciously, sold her to the English. We, even more ungraciously, set fire to her and threw her ashes into the River Seine (a fine way to treat a lady). Her spirit lived on, however, and the French won back the whole lot again apart from — wait for it – Calais, which I suppose served us right. Mind you, if you've ever been to Calais you'd know why the French didn't want it. As for Joan, however, everything turned out all right in the end. Twenty years after her execution she was

retried (unfortunately she couldn't be there) by Pope Calixtus III and found not guilty. In 1920 she was made a saint. So you see, all things come to those who wait!

1455 – War of the Roses

As young Henry got older it became fairly obvious that he had a screw loose like his grandad. Luckily, his wife Margaret was quite a tough cookie so that when the next war arrived she did the business for him. This came in 1455 and seemed to be about whether red roses were nicer than white ones. Margaret and the Lancastrians (the famous band) seemed to like red ones and the Duke of York and the Earl of Warwick favoured white.

1461 – Edward IV

Poor Henry the Daft got collared by the whites and the Duke of York got captured and murdered by the reds. The new Duke of

51

York got crowned Edward IV in 1461. The last huge battle occurred at Towton (No! not Toytown) where the Yorkists beat the Lancastrians good and proper. Henry, who was now out-to-lunch brainwise, ended up in the Bloody Tower (bloody shame) and was – you've got it, now – murdered.

As most of the noblemen who'd controlled Parliament had either been killed or executed, Edward got all their cash – King's perk! This caused no end of strife and his friend Warwick, who'd helped make him king, teamed up with Margaret (remember her? the tough one), and fought the new king at Barnet in a fog which seems

a rather strange place to do battle. Warwick fell off his horse, and because his armour was so heavy, couldn't move. He was badly killed and the battle was lost. Queen Margaret, her son and hubby six feet under, sloped off to France where she died in poverty.

Edward, being the true heir to Richard II, became the new flavour of the month. He had a high old time in London; so much so that he died in 1483 from sloth and over indulgence. Sounds all right to me!

52

1483 – Edward V

His elder son Edward V was only twelve years old and was 'protected' by his wicked uncle Gloucester who had ideas of his own. Gloucester claimed that the king and his brother were illegitimate and had them smothered in the Tower (see bad places to spend a night). Their skeletons were found in an old wooden box many years later, and only positively identified in 1933.

Some modern historians now say old Gloucester didn't do it and that he probably wasn't such a bad bloke at all.

1483 – Richard III

He became the infamous Richard III, a horrid chap who managed to cut the heads off just about everyone. He was universally hated especially by Henry (Lord of the Lancasters) who fought him at Bosworth. Richard, who jauntily sported his crown into battle got the worst of it and at one point offered his kingdom for a horse. As

deals go, I don't think that's bad. Unfortunately, they didn't carry a spare and Richard was slain. His body was subjected to 'many indignities' (the mind boggles) and Henry picked up the crown, shoved it on his head, and became the VII, the first Tudor, in 1485.

1485 – Henry VII

When he married Edward IV's daughter Elizabeth, the Yorks and the Lancasters were united and it was generally agreed that red roses weren't any better than white ones. The War of the Roses was officially called a draw.

By the Way

Richard's naked body was taken to Leicester where it was displayed for two days at Greyfriars (no Billy Bunter jokes please!). When Greyfriars was dissolved they rather ignominiously chucked his body into the river.

Meanwhile

1376 – John Wycliff and the Lollards denounced the Pope and demanded reforms.

1378 – Two Popes at Rome and Avignon had a huge tiff and stopped talking.

1400 – Middle English gave birth to modern English.

1415 – Oil colours introduced into painting.

1430 – 'Mad Marjorie' a huge cast iron gun scared everyone.

1440 – Gutenberg, a German inventor printed from the first movable type.

1465 – First printed music. Sorry, don't know what the tune was.

1477 – Our boy Caxton printed *Canterbury Tales*.

Chapter 15:

Watch Out, There's A Henry About

Everyone then agreed to end the Middle Ages along with serfs, villeins and the feudal system. In fact, dukes also nearly ended because there was only one left. The invention of gunpowder made armour and castles useless and, as the king was the only one who could afford lots of cannons, it made rebelling a bit iffy.

Everyone at this time was rushing round the world (chaps like Chris Columbus), discovering new countries. I think they always

I THINK THAT'S AMERICA.

COLUMBUS LTD. DISCOVERERS

had, but the invention of maps and compasses meant they could at last get back to tell someone. The English started to get much cleverer owing to a rediscovery of Greek literature. Funny, the Greeks seem to have lost it! William Caxton discovered the book (but don't ask where), and most people read it. At this time there were 4,000,000 people living here quite peacefully as Henry had done away with private armies – and still (much more to the point) he had the best weapons. Also he had pots of his own money so didn't have to tax everyone as much.

His smartest move was to marry his daughter to the son of James II (King of Scotland) and his son Arthur to Catherine of Aragon, whose dad was King of Spain. When young Arthur died in 1502, Catherine was passed on to his younger brother Henry. I dread to think what the Women's Movement would have had to say about that.

Henry VII still had a bit of aggro from the remaining Yorkies, but generally left the country rich and peaceful when he died in 1509.

1509 – Henry VIII

The world famous Henry VIII became king at eighteen. He was an athlete, poet, musician, patron of the arts (and all round clever

Dick). He wasn't a bit like his dad and soon started giving the French a hard time again but with little success. Henry spent most of his money on a huge navy, greatly encouraged by Thomas Wolsey, Archbishop of York, Cardinal and Chancellor who had almost as much cash as the king.

1509 – Wife No. 1

Now, as you remember Henry was married to his dead brother's wife – or should that be ex-wife – Catherine the Spanish girl. The trouble was, he thought she was knocking on a bit, especially as all their five children were daughters and four of them unfortunately dead. As he fancied a son (and a housemaid called Anne), he decided to claim that the marriage was invalid – nice one, Henry – and got Wolsey to ask the Pope to let him off. The Pope, who was under the King of Spain's thumb, refused. Henry, therefore, cheekily told him where to get off and made himself head of the Church. Two outstanding heads of Church and State, Bishop Fisher and Sir Thomas More, wouldn't go along with it so Henry

promptly had their heads off. Thomas's poor head was apparently parboiled, stuck on a pole, and exhibited on London Bridge. His daughter bribed the bridge-keeper to knock it down and she, being a good catch, nicked it and took it home. Years later, when dead herself, she was buried with it.

56

1532 – Wife No. 2

Henry married Anne Boleyn and later charged Wolsey with extremely high treason which is a fine way to treat your mates!

He then appointed Thomas Cromwell to replace Wolsey and together they 'dissolved' all the monasteries (probably in Holy Water) and took all the Church's assets, as at that time the Church owned about a quarter of the country. The Pope went do-lally and excommunicated him, but Henry just laughed and said 'Go forth and multiply'! This became the beginning of the Reformation which was the biggest shake-down the Church had ever seen. Anyone who didn't agree with Henry was called a heretic and promptly burned. Most people tended to like it!

Anne, unfortunately, gave him yet another daughter (Elizabeth) in 1533. This really put Henry's back up, but not as much as her flirting with the courtiers. When he found out, he chopped not only her head off, but all her supposed lovers' (plural) heads too. It's interesting to note that Anne was a bit of a freak, having an extra finger on one hand, and – even more weird – three breasts. If the

adultery and incest (with her brother) charges hadn't stuck, Henry planned to have her charged as a witch, using her deformities as evidence. It really wasn't Anne's year, for after being executed her heart was stolen and secretly hidden. It was found again in 1836 and buried under the church organ in Thetford, Suffolk. The current vicar's favourite song is reported to be 'You Gotta Have Heart'.

1536 – Wife No. 3

Next up was Jane Seymour who – good news – bore him a son, but – bad news – died in 1537 doing so. Tudor surgery, unfortunately, wasn't up to much.

He then tried to marry his sister's baby granddaughter, Mary (one day Queen of Scots), but the Scottish nobles wouldn't have it (quite right too!).

1540 – Wife No. 4

Now it was the turn of Anne of Cleves, 'The Flemish Mare'. Although she was remarkably ugly, it was generally reckoned to be politically a good idea. The marriage wasn't consummated (ask your parents) and he soon divorced her. He obviously wasn't too fond of horses (Flemish Mare?). Poor Cromwell got the chop because the marriage had been his idea. That's what happens if you do your friend a favour.

1540 – Wife No. 5

Henry then tried another maid-in-waiting, Catherine Howard, but she was a bit too bright for him so, true to form, he chopped her head off (an occupational hazard).

1543 – Wife No. 6

I bet Katherine Parr, Henry's last wife, was nervous on the wedding day. By this time Henry was in a terrible physical state and some of his afflictions were too disgusting to relate (which, believe me, is pretty disgusting) so Katherine outlived him. He died in 1547 aged fifty-six leaving a country, though broke from constant wars, more confident than ever before.

Meanwhile

1473–1543 – Copernicus reckoned that we were all going round the sun (and round the bend).

1489	– Symbols + and – came into use.
1494	– Whisky distilled in Scotland.
1498	– The Chinese discovered the toothbrush and had the best smiles.
1500	– Martin Luther, famous Protestant reformer, was one of the first people to have had a candle-lit Christmas Tree in his front room.
1503	– Noses blown all over Britain owing to the popularity of the handkerchief. I suppose that up to that time they must have used their sleeves.
1503	– Leonardo da Vinci painted his grumpy girlfriend Mona (Lisa).
1508	– Pope told Michelangelo to give the Sistine Chapel ceiling a coat of paint.
1517	– Coffee came to Europe.
1520	– Chocolate followed (at last).
1521	– Martin Luther (not King) condemned as a heretic and excommunicated.
1522	– Magellan set off across the world and proved it was round by coming back to the same place.
1533	– First lunatic asylums (but by no means the first loonies).
1547	– Terrible Ivan (The Terrible) crowned tsar of Russia.

Chapter 16:

Are You Ready, Eddie? – 1547

All this bonhomie and prosperity fell to bits in the next decade owing to the constant argy-bargy between the Catholics and the Protestants.

Poor little Edward VI (Henry's lad) became king aged nine and didn't know what to do for the best. He was helped by his uncle Somerset, a staunch Protestant, along with Thomas Cranmer (even stauncher). The economy took a nose dive until the Treasury was as empty as a politician's promise. Unemployment was rife and the country became totally cheesed off. Sounds a little familiar, doesn't it?

When the Duke of Northumberland took over from Somerset, he realised that the only cash left belonged to the Protestant Church which was now flavour of the month. He stripped the churches of all their good bits and left them with just a chalice and a bell (very big of him!).

Funnily enough, although he wasn't too struck on God, he made everyone else go to church. If they didn't, he fined or imprisoned them. Attendances improved miraculously (Church of England take note). When Northumberland spotted that the adolescent king was permanently looking a little peaky, and possibly not long for this world, he made his son Dudley marry Lady Jane Grey, a cousin of old Henry VII (the one with all the cannons). He sneakily bullied Edward into leaving her everything, including the crown, in his will. The first bit he got right, as the king snuffed it in 1553, but the rest of the plan was screwed up.

1553 – Lady Jane Grey

Lady Jane only managed to hang onto the crown for nine days before she and poor Dudley were found some rooms in the Tower. The British, fed up to the back teeth with Protestant rule, had said no way, as they were greedy, corrupt, and couldn't run a booze-up in a brewery. They wanted Mary, daughter of Catherine of Aragon (first Mrs of Henry VIII), and got their way.

1553 – Mary Tudor

Mary Tudor turned out to be exactly what they didn't want. She was stroppy, inflexible and about as much fun as a wet Sunday. She thought God had sent for her to bring England back to Catholicism – here we go again. She married King Philip of Spain (free holidays?) and so brought England back (protestanting) under the Pope. Just to make things neat and tidy, she executed Lady Jane and her new hubby. I bet Dudley cursed his dad. After all, the marriage was his daft idea.

Then she set about barbecuing the Protestants at Smithfield – later, rather appropriately, a meat market. First she sent to the stake (or maybe steak) all the bishops, followed by anyone she could get her flames on. It was reliably reported that as Latimer, Bishop of Oxford, was waiting for his turn, he said these famous words, 'We shall this day light such a candle by God's grace in England as, I trust, shall never be put out'. Unfortunately, they lit him instead (and didn't put him out!). It seems there was a daily fry up for nearly a year. You couldn't do it now because they don't allow bonfires in central London.

So England became a province of Spain (olé) which made all us English-hombres muchos mad. They even made us join in their bloody war with France and guess what? We lost Calais. Mary was disgraced and died of extreme grumpiness in 1558 aged forty-two. England, to show its respect, had a huge, drunken party to celebrate.

Chapter 17

Good Queen Bess – 1558

Elizabeth was the daughter of Anne Boleyn (see headless mums) and reckoned by the Catholics to be illegitimate. She was twenty-five when 'queened' and a rather plain, skinny sort, with bright red hair like her dad's. Her looks weren't improved by the use of a form of white, lead-based make-up which, although fashionable, had a rather unfortunate habit of eating into one's face. It's worth noting, that in those days people never washed or changed their underclothes, so they often carried a cloved apple to disguise the pong (how pleasant). Elizabeth tried to compensate for her rather offputting personal features by wearing 'over the top' clothes the like of which had never been seen before.

Unfortunately, she had inherited a right mess. England was skint, divided, weak and surrounded by a bunch of extremely unpleasant enemies. To cap that, half the country thought Mary Queen of Scots should rule even though Scotland was now French. Lizzie, luckily, was as bright as a button and fortunately didn't give a damn which religion God wanted her subjects to be. She'd really

had enough of the Catholics, however, so promptly told the Pope and the Spanish where to go, and set about making everyone in England friends and Protestants again.

She then helped Scotland give the French 'le grande elbow' in 1559. The Frogs were so dejected, having a civil war of their own, that they were to be as good as gold for years.

1568 – Spanish Trouble

Spain was a different matter. They threatened us with Armadas (nasty gangs of warships) every five minutes. Elizabeth was a gutsy lady, however, and didn't scare easily. She and her advisors set about getting the country back on its feet, inventing apprenticeships, relief for the poor (what a relief), and work for the unemployed. There was an enormous expansion in trade and manufacture and by 1568 England was back on its feet (Elizabeth II and Thatcher 1st take note!).

This was the year that Francis Drake aged twenty-eight set off for the New World with his chum, Sir John Hawkins, a second-hand slave salesman. Also this year, Mary (ex-Queen of Scots), was chased out of Scotland for marrying the guy that blew her husband up. In the rush to England she forgot her baby who then had to be King of Scotland (James VI).

Elizabeth was strangely unsympathetic and kept her virtually imprisoned. Of course it just could have had something to do with the Spanish constantly plotting to get Mary on the English throne. Never quite sure of just what they were cooking up she eventually cut Mary's head off in 1587 which seemed to do the trick nicely. The famous drink Bloody Mary was aptly named after her.

1588 – Spanish Armada

As you can imagine, her execution rather annoyed the Spanish who decided to invade us at last. Drake, who'd been having a ball robbing and plundering the Spanish merchant ships, became top hero when he snuck into Cadiz harbour and burnt most of Philip of

Spain's parked invasion fleet. When the Armada finally pitched up in English waters their huge lumbering galleons were outwitted by our nippy little ones. Add to that a teriffic storm which destroyed half their ships, and you can guess the result. The final score was one small ship to them and seventy-two great big 'uns to us. The 'Invincible' Armada returned to Spain with its sails between its legs.

The Elizabethans

While all this was going on, everyone was having a high old time in England. The Elizabethan Age had arrived. Elizabeth had a boyfriend called Essex (not David) and Shakespeare, the new hit writer, had his head well down, furiously scribbling plays. The

OUT DAMN SPOT.

English were reckoned to be the best musicians in Europe, even without a Eurovision Song Contest, and most certainly the most contented nation (those were the days). At last, thanks to Elizabeth, we were united under a common law, a common bible, a Book of Common Prayer, a common literature and a common language. (It all sounds far too common for my liking.)

Lizzie's other favourite was Sir Walter Raleigh who became famous for:

1. Introducing the potato to the Irish (they became instant friends).

2. Living in the Tower of London for twelve years without being murdered.
3. Showing the Queen how to walk on water without getting her feet wet (Jesus please note).
4. Bringing tobacco to England (it's all his fault).
5. Not finding the golden city of Eldorado.
6. Being executed in 1618.
7. Having his head kept in a leather bag (red) by his wife for twenty-nine years.

Good Queen Bess died in 1603, still a virgin, having rather stupidly cut off the boyfriend's head.

Chapter 18:

Two Kings For The Price Of One – 1603

James was the I of England and the VI of Scotland. He was the poor little perisher left as a baby by Mary his mummy when she had to leave in rather a hurry. He came down to London aged thirty-seven and was the first ever king of all the four countries of the British Isles. He was, overall, a peaceful sort of chap which suited the England that Elizabeth had left behind. There were hardly any murders, no feuds, no bandits and only a little war with Spain. James sorted the latter out fairly quickly and everything looked to be going OK, apart from – surprise, surprise – religion. At this time there were three denominations in England. The Anglicans (invented by Lizzie), The Roman Catholics, and the Puritans (hard-line Protestants). These last were a strange bunch who thought that anything that approached looking like fun was wicked (and quite right too!). They hated theatre, dancing, ornamentation and smiling.

1605 – Guy Fawkes
These three were always arguing. It became so heated that one day a guy called Guido Fawkes (a Catholic) accidentally invented Bonfire night by nearly blowing up the Anglican Parliament. Just imagine how much more famous (and popular) he'd have been if he'd actually got away with it. (Come back Guido, all is forgiven).

1610 – Distant Lands
James personally hated the Puritans and finally lost his rag and told

them that if they didn't conform to the Anglican church they could jolly well get lost. They took the hint and set out in a boat called the *Mayflower* to try to find Virginia. They got a bit lost, but did find America. Rather cheekily, they named the bit that they eventually landed on, New England (which it still is).

1613 – Funny Goings-On

James, although a bit clever, was thought to be coarse, scruffy, gross, and very cocky. He preferred the 'company' of men to women and proved it by making his special boyfriend, Buckingham, the first ever non-Royal duke. His whole court was a bit suspect

(nudge nudge, wink wink), and at one point in 1619 his former Lord Chamberlain, Lord Treasurer, Secretary of State and Captain of the Gentlemen Pensioners (sounds like a geriatric cricket team), were all banged up in the Tower. They were accused of various sexual or financial offences, which I'd prefer not to go into.

Britain at this time was the last of the European countries to rush overseas to set up colonies and trading stations in far distant lands. This was probably because our boats were a bit clapped out

following the Spanish war and James had been too tight with his cash to patch them up. Our first proper colony, however, was in Virginia and our first proper trading outfit was called the East India Company.

When James I finally called it a day in 1625 he left huge debts, an unsavoury court and a nice new war with Spain.

By the Way

Guy Fawkes had ten accomplices. When the Gunpowder Plot was discovered Guy was caught (and horribly executed) while the others escaped to a 'safe' house in Staffordshire. They arrived soaked to the skin and decided to dry their socks by the fire. While chucking on an extra log, a stray spark ignited the gunpowder they were still carrying. Several were maimed and blinded, and the blast attracted the attention of pursuing soldiers who promptly massacred the rest.

Meanwhile

1562 – Milled coins introduced. It appears some naughty chaps had been amassing gold and silver by clipping bits off the coins.

1565 – First graphite pencils.

1589 – Sir John Harington installed the first proper water closet (lavatory). Bet he was popular with his chums.

1596 – Galileo invented the thermometer – and found out he had a temperature!

1600 – Dutch opticians invented the telescope.

1611 – King James allowed each colonist in Jamestown, Virginia, to be given gardens to grow hemp as a fibre source. It was known, even then, that the top leaves of the hemp plant, when dried, produce hashish or cannabis – an intoxicating drug.

1619 – William Harvey discovered blood – and how it goes round us.

1624 – A crazy Dutchman, Cornelius Drebble, stretched some greased leather round a wooden frame and when it didn't float realised he'd discovered the submarine.

Chapter 19:

What! A Charlie? – 1625

Charles I (crowned in 1625) couldn't have been less like his dad if he'd tried. A right little runt (5ft 4ins) who was prudish, shy, shifty and st-stammering. If his father never really understood the English, Charlie never really understood anyone at all. He believed that if he set a good example, the world would follow. How wrong could he be. The first daft thing he did was marry Henrietta, the King of Spain's daughter, which really got up the nose of all the non-Catholics. With the help of his chief adviser, the Duke of Buckingham, handsome ex-boyfriend of his ex-dad, Charles managed to intensify the war.

1625 – War With Spain

He asked Parliament for money to fight with and they told him to get lost. Weedy Charles tried to do it on the cheap without them, but soon got into a right mess. He begged them again, and again they told him to go away – but probably not that politely. He then tried to borrow money off his friends. Cheekier still, he forced

people to feed his troops for free, throwing them into jail if they refused. Parliament eventually gave in and told him that if he was a good boy and behaved himself, they'd give him the cash. He blew it all though, and was forced, finally, to crawl to the Spanish king and make peace (what a Charlie!).

1629 – Trouble With Parliament

Charles was one of those kings who thought he was next in line to God, which meant nobody had the right to question him. This really peeved the patient Parliament. In the end things came to the crunch over – three guesses – religion again. Parliament passed a resolution against the Catholic faith which Charles, having Catholic sympathies, took rather badly. He sent them all packing and ran the country alone for eleven years. If you're wondering what happened to the beautiful Buckingham, he was assassinated by 'a ten-penny knife' owned by an obscure lieutenant, cross at not being promoted.

1635 – Civil War Looms

Charles was still strapped for cash so he taxed the wealthy landowners heavily, and, for reasons best known to himself, anyone who lived by or near the sea (the Ship Tax). Then he stuck his nose into Scottish religion, which miffed them so much they invaded England (so far – so good, Charlie!). Very few of his soldiers could be bothered to fight so he called a Parliament again in 1640 to

force them. Parliament refused and executed his two best advisers for luck, the whizz kid Earl of Strafford and William Laud, which again made Charles mad. He took what was left of his army to arrest them all in London, but they all hid. The whole country took sides and whoopee! we have a proper civil war (nice one, Charles!).

The Sides

The Roundheads	vs	The Cavaliers
Parliament		The King
The Commons		Catholics
The Puritans		The High Churchmen
Industrial areas		Most Lords
Navy and Ports		Old Gentry
London		The North and West
The East and South		Oxford

Although the Cavaliers – another word for swaggerers – initially had the most muscle, the Roundheads – so called because of their short haircuts – soon caught up and overtook. Parliament had much better access to funds by taxing everyone like crazy. They did a sneaky deal with Scotland, promising them that they'd let England become Presbyterian (National Church of Scotland) if they helped fight the king. What really decided the whole shooting match was one man, a Puritan called Oliver Cromwell, MP for Cambridge.

1640 – Witches

It was also the time of the famous witch-hunts. Anything that went wrong in the countryside – bad crops, hens not laying, wives becoming ugly, etc. was blamed on witches. Any single old woman who had a broom and/or a cat was suspected of witchcraft. A nasty piece of work called Matthew Hopkins toured Merrie England for three years from 1644, killing old women willy-nilly. His best test involved throwing the poor old souls into any convenient pond. If they sank they were innocent and if they floated it meant Satan was helping them so they were guilty and promptly burned. It was heads

I THINK WE JUST MIGHT HAVE MADE A MISTAKE.

you lose, tails you lose. Hopkins became so good at witch-spotting (sure beats train-spotting) that, in the end, people wondered if Satan wasn't on his side and hanged him as well for good measure.

1642 – Oliver Cromwell

Cromwell started out drilling volunteers for the Parliamentary party, but soon emerged as one of their top men. In 1644 a combination of Roundheads, Scots and Cromwell's new cavalry beat the pants off the Cavaliers or Royalists at Marston Moor. This gained him loads of Brownie points and Parliament was so chuffed that they asked Cromwell to build a flash new elite army of professional soldiers. It was called the New Model Army and the men were paid the unheard of sum of 10p a day. These guys were mostly 'Independents' as they hated the Anglicans and the Presbyterians. Though damn tough, they were a right bunch of

'SCUSE ME – COULD I SEE YOUR HAIRCUT.

goody-goodies (though you wouldn't have dared tell them), trained not to drink, swear, rape or pillage. When it came to fighting, however, they were fab and beat the undisciplined Cavaliers wherever they came up against them.

Charles, seeing he was getting the worst of it, scarpered up to Scotland in 1646 thinking he'd get well looked after as his old man was once their king. No such luck. The Scots, never ones to miss the chance of filling their sporrans, promptly flogged him to Parliament — For Sale, one King!

Cromwell, who was by then Parliament's blue-eyed boy, was given £2,500 a year commission for fixing the deal. Lots of the Royalist soldiers, stuck without a leader and no wages, sloped home to their wives.

Roundheads

Things weren't too clever with the Roundheads either. Parliament was continually harassing them, and worse, sacking their no-longer-needed army without paying them. Cromwell was well brassed off, so he seized poor Charles and offered him a generous deal.

As a result of Cromwell's actions civil war broke out between Cromwell's rough, tough army and a weird combination of the English Presbyterians, the surly Scots and what was left of the Royalists. In 1648 Cromwell's heavies beat them hollow at the Battle of Preston. Ollie then high-tailed it down to London and gave all the Presbyterians in Parliament the boot.

1648 – The Rump

This left just sixty Independents rather daftly called 'the Rump'. Cromwell then did his naughtiest thing ever. He tried the king for high treason and then in 1649, at a huge public ceremony, neatly severed his head (a rather disloyal thing to do to your king).

He nothing common did or mean
Upon that memorable scene . . .
But bow'd his comely head
Down as upon a bed.
Andrew Marvell (Ode to Cromwell)

MIND YOUR
FINGERS

Very noble I'm sure, but it looks as if poor old Charlie didn't have much choice.

MY! WHAT A
CHARMING LITTLE
SALT-CELLAR.

Not many folk know that when Charles's coffin was rediscovered in 1813, the Royal surgeon, Sir Henry Halford, did an autopsy on the body and nicked poor Charles's fourth vertebra. For years he used to horrify his mates by using it as a salt holder at dinner parties. Queen Victoria, never one to like a joke, ordered him to put it back in the coffin.

Meanwhile, although Charles had never been exactly a fave rave, the Brits didn't take too well to someone chopping their king's head off. In those days, however, if you'd had enough of the government

74

(and we all know how that feels), you couldn't just moan about your leaders in the local take-away. Telling tales on people was a national sport, and public execution a great day out for all the family, providing it wasn't your turn. Part of the army eventually mutinied, followed by the navy. This situation intrigued 'abroad', who were always waiting on the sidelines for any opportunity to attack us.

Chapter 20:

Look Out, Charles – 1650

Meanwhile up at Scone (remember? We've still got their stone!) the Scots were crowning Charles's son, Charles II, who'd been in Holland hiding in the Hague. Cromwell was solving his problems as only he knew how. He shot the mutineers, invaded and massacred the revolting Irish and only then turned his attention to Scotland and their brand new king. It took a few bloody battles to show the Royalist Scots who was boss. Charles, who'd apparently spent much of his time hiding up a tree (funny lot, kings!), rather wisely went on a prolonged holiday to France in 1651 and I bet he didn't send any postcards.

EARLY SANDCASTLE

Cromwell kindly gave his soldiers, who'd all got nasty colds and flu, a nice rest. He then built up the navy and thumbed his nose at all our foreign enemies who'd missed their chance to get us while our trousers were down, so to speak. It wasn't long before we ruled the seas again and Cromwell's tough-guy sailor boys got back some of our colonies he'd lost by blowing away the king.

1653 – King Oliver?

Oliver obviously wasn't someone who was easy to get on with, and before long he fell out with his Rump, which sounds rather painful. He fired the lot of them and so, for the first time, England was ruled by a military dictatorship.

Some slimy creeps kept begging him to become king, but Oliver didn't fancy it much and who blames him. Instead of being King Olly I he called himself the 'Lord Protector of a United Commonwealth of England, Scotland, Ireland and the Colonies' (what a mouthful).

By the Way

Cromwell died of natural causes, believe it or not, aged sixty. Just before he was buried, his brain was weighed and found to be an incredible 82.25 ounces (the average man's weighs 49 ounces).

Some time later, when definitely wormbait, he was dug up (pooh!) with all his fellow king killers and strung up at Tyburn. As a special treat, Cromwell's head was displayed on a pole outside Westminster Abbey which jolly well served him right – not, I suspect, that he cared. It remained there for twenty-four years until

1685 when a strong wind blew it off. It was found by a captain of the guard who took it home and hid it up his chimney. Years later it turned up at a freak show and was valued at sixty guineas. An actor, Samuel Russell, had been paying his rent by charging the punters half a crown a look. After changing hands several more times it ended up on display in Bond Street. The syndicate which had bought it for £230 all died mysteriously and it fell into the hands of a Doctor Wilkinson. The Wilkinson family kept it in a wooden box, wrapped in red and black silk, for years and years until eventually giving it to Sydney Sussex College in 1960 where it was buried secretly.

Chapter 21:

Come Back, Charlie – 1660

After a bit more light anarchy, someone called up Charles II, probably on a French beach, and told him it was all right to come home. This he did forthwith and arrived by 'Hovership' at Dover in May 1660, aged thirty, now more French than English and probably sporting a beret.

The British went crazy and had a high old time. Life under Cromwell had not been exactly a barrel of laughs. Everyone was really looking forward to being quite the opposite of a Puritan or Quaker (same sort of thing). Britain was by now, despite everything, ever so rich and important and all those frightful foreigners had become quite scared of us (not like now – eh!).

Good-Time Charlie

Charles, I'm afraid, only came back to have a good time. Although witty, carefree, and a good laugh (if you were his pal), he was also totally selfish and unscrupulous and dead ugly. He wasn't, strangely enough, that keen on continuing to give the Catholics a hard time and set about making friends. He married a rather prim and proper Portuguese princess called Catherine of Braganza but, being a lecherous young chappie, spent most of his time with his many mistresses and millions of illegitimate kids. One of his famous girlfriends was a certain Nell Gwynne, an orange salesperson, famed for the size and quality of her – oranges!

Plague Again

It was during his reign that Britain had a nasty dose of the plague again. In London alone, 700,000 poor devils died. It wasn't really surprising because London was a filthy place with garbage piled in the streets and lots of people sleeping rough (so what's changed?). If it was suspected that anyone in your house was feeling a little poorly, your neighbours would paint a nice red cross on your door and then nail it shut with you and your family inside. The drag was, if it wasn't the plague, then you'd damn well starve to death instead.

If anyone did manage to escape the city to stay with relatives in the country, the simple rural folk weren't that sympathetic. They'd either murder you or cut off any village suspected of having the plague until you, and everyone else, perished.

Top of the Pops that year was a little song that went:

A ring, a ring of roses (the red spots on your body)
A pocket full of posies (thought to keep the infection away)
Atishoo! Atishoo! (the first symptom)
We all fall down (speaks for itself!)

1666 – The Great Fire

Just as the Londoners were getting over this lot, a daft baker in Pudding Lane accidentally set fire to his shop (he should have used his loaf) and started the Great Fire of London. You could say it never rains but it pours, but unfortunately it had been a real scorcher of a summer and they hadn't seen a spot – apart from red ones – for ages. As the houses were all made of wood, the inferno swept through the streets like 'the Roadrunner' and in the seven days that it lasted, 10,000 houses and eighty churches were destroyed. Fortunately, only six people were killed, but that could have been because the plague took the rest the year before.

1668 – Puritan Bashing!

Meanwhile Charles's first Parliament was really giving a lot of stick to the remaining Puritans. They weren't allowed to hold high office (serves 'em right) and if they met for religious reasons or showed their faces in the towns, they were promptly thrown into jail or transported to the colonies, which, all things considered, sounds like the safest place to have been.

Not only was there another big conflagration a year later but, to put the tin lid on it, the daring Dutch, with more than a little Dutch courage, sailed right up the Thames and set fire to our brill fleet. Charles's most faithful servant, the Earl of Clarendon, somehow got the blame for all this lot (someone's always the scapegoat) and was himself fired from running the government. Charles, meanwhile, had a real ace up his sleeve. He did a brilliantly tricky secret deal with Louis XIV of France. Believe it or not, he promised old Louis that in return for £1,200,000 a year cash in hand, he would help fight the Dutch (revenge is sweet) and also try to make England Catholic again. Parliament went barmy when it found out, and told him – NO WAY! They made Charles sign a Test Act excluding any Catholic from high office. It was a bit embarrassing, because this meant that his brother, the heir to the throne, James – Duke of York, was also excluded as he was a Catholic too.

1678 – Titus Oates

A real rascal called Titus Oates (I wonder if he was a Quaker?) reckoned he'd heard of a Catholic plot to top the king and put James on the throne. As usual, no-one checked the story and panic set in. Lots of poor, innocent Catholics were executed just on Oates's say so. A new Parliament passed an act to prevent James ever being king. The supporters of the act were called Whigs, and those who didn't – Tories (sounds familiar).

1681 – Which King Next?

Civil war loomed again, but Charles being always ahead of the game, managed to keep all the balls in the air by ruling without Parliament. Remember, he was still getting a great pay-off from France. The joke was, that it was France which was becoming number one threat, not Holland as before. The trouble with the Whigs was that although they couldn't bear the idea of James on the throne, they couldn't make up their minds who they did want. It was a toss up between Monmouth, known rather unkindly as the 'Royal Bastard' or Mary, James's Protestant daughter.

This terrible, but admittedly, peaceful indecision allowed the Tories to become much stronger and they eventually hounded many of the leading Whigs to death. Soon there were none left in Parliament. James, meanwhile, was going crazy in Scotland taking it out on the Presbyterians in the vilest manner.

In the end Charles II totally won the day and died happy in 1685. He left a country ruled by Tories who believed the king knew best, the Church knew second best and all the localities knew third best.

Chapter 22

Hanging Around In 1685

If England had thought that James II was just what they'd always been looking for – he wasn't. Despite telling them all he was a good guy, in his heart of hearts he was a real fanatic. He'd had an unconventional royal childhood eventually running away to France, dressed as a girl (no comment), to serve with the French army. When he became king the English Protestants were terrified, as French Protestants were turning up on our shores telling gruesome stories of what was happening to their mates being persecuted by Louis XIV, James's old chum. Their fears weren't helped by James keeping a huge menacing army on the outskirts of London.

PARDON MADAMOISELLE. WE DON'T TAKE GIRLS.

FRANCE

1685 – Monmouth Turns Up

Things got off to an exciting start when his old rival for the throne, Monmouth, arrived in Lyme Regis with a weedy little army that was knocked into the middle of the next week by James's bully boys. This was the very last proper battle in England (apart from last year's F.A. cup tie).

Monmouth's execution was a particularly messy affair, as it took five chops (ouch!). Just as they were about to bury the two bits some bright spark realised that there wasn't a proper portrait of the ex-Duke. As he was the illegitimate son of Charles II they thought they'd better get one done. They therefore sewed his head back on his body, put him back in his clothes, sat him in a chair and, Bob's your uncle – one picture! If you don't believe me, the portrait's still hanging in the National Portrait Gallery, London.

1686 – Judge Jeffreys

One of James's employees, a nice chap called Judge Jeffreys, thought of an original way to decorate the streets. His job had been to try Monmouth's rebels on 'the Bloody Western Circuit'. To say he was strict was a bit of an understatement. He deported 800 rebels to the West Indies and Barbados not, I hasten to add, for the good of their health and the 300 left were dangled along the sides

of the roads as an example to others. (They must have got the message, wouldn't you?) Neither the Whigs nor the Tories were too pleased by James's cruelty but with his army of 30,000 professional soldiers behind him it was tough bananas!

Although James was always trying to get his mates the Catholics into the best jobs, he was tolerated because Parliament knew that when he died, his Protestant daughter, Mary, would take over. Everyone was gobsmacked therefore, when James's second Mrs – Mary Beatrice, really put the cat (or brat) amongst the pigeons (or Anglicans) by having a blasted boy (and not a bastard boy) after ten years of baby-free marriage.

1688 – William and Mary

Suddenly for once, everyone agreed and decided to ask William of Orange – James's nephew (and daughter Mary's hubby) – to come and have a nice friendly chat to try and talk James out of making Britain's future, Catholic (fat chance).

What actually happened was rather bizarre. William arrived with 500 ships and 14,000 'friendly' troops who came ashore at Brixham in 1688 and turned right towards London. James led his huge army towards them but started having terrible nosebleeds which tended to hold up the marching. He became increasingly peculiar and seemed to be going round the bend. Many of his officers and commanders thought 'blow this for a game of soldiers' and slipped away. James completely lost his bottle and ran back to London, soon to be caught up by a rather puzzled William. Had James not been a bit do-lally he could still have saved the situation. But no – not him. He just ran away with his son, only a nipper, to France where Louis XIV was really pleased to have them, as he was looking for any excuse to attack England. As James was leaving he dropped the Great Seal of England, the symbol of authority, into the Thames hoping it could hinder the running of the country. This didn't hinder anything, however (and the seal was probably happier anyway). From that moment he was considered to have jacked in the throne.

The Whigs and Tories seemed rather relieved and let Mr and Mrs Orange be their king and queen. So ended what came to be known as the Bloodless Revolution.

Chapter 23:

Oranges Are Good For You — 1689

William and Mary were crowned in 1689 and the British, who always liked a change, were delighted. William had been a sort of King of Holland and had become a bit of a hero shooing off the French who'd been trying to invade. He did this, rather cleverly, by opening all the dykes and flooding most of Holland apart from

Amsterdam — where he lived. This soaked the French and sent them swimming home. Fine, if all you want to rule is a lake, but I think his action defines the term 'cutting off your nose to spite your face'!

This Bloodless or Glorious Revolution, was important because it was the first time that Parliament had decided who should succeed to the throne. This, of course, suddenly made it jolly important, and although the Crown had to approve its measures, Parliament gained a power that it was never again to lose.

Another first, was the right to worship however and whoever you wanted without the fear of having your head parted from your body.

1689 — England United
It should be said that although England was feeling united, there were only 5,000,000 of us and 20,000,000 of those blasted French. Louis still reckoned James was our king, though I fail to see what business it was of his, and was prepared, at the drop of a crown, to fight to put him on the throne again.

Strangely enough Scotland, for once, supported England – apart from some horrible Highlanders who were promptly 'killied' at Killiecrankie. There wasn't a welcome either from the MacDonald clan of Glencoe who took far too long making up their minds whose side they were on. They were unfortunately made into Big Macs by the English, who just couldn't wait.

1690 – The Irish

The Irish, always ones to be difficult, decided to support James and invited King Louis over to form a Catholic army to fight the English. They decided first to besiege and then rout the remaining Protestants in Londonderry (a bit like the IRA are trying to do now). 'Orange Billy', as he was known, called up his old Dutch mates, who still thought the French were creeps, and an Anglo-Dutch Army met the O'Frogs on the banks of the Boyne in 1690. Although short, pock marked, weedy, asthmatic and anaemic, William stayed in the saddle for nine-teen hours. His army crushed the French who, probably fed up with the dreadful Irish cuisine (potatoes and more potatoes), went home. The poor old Irish Catholics lost everything including the right to be educated (no Irish jokes – please!).

1690 – War with France No. 1

A Frenchman, like an elephant, never forgets, and we were soon at proper war with France. Wars were now evolving into something different, however, as soldiers from whichever side were beginning to dislike being killed in great numbers. Sieges were much more fun. All you had to do was sit around some city or encampment, smoking, drinking and waving your weapons around every now and again, while the ones inside did the same. The winner was the side that didn't get bored first. This is a simplification of course, but you get the idea.

Anyway that was how this particular war with the French was 'fought' so it tended to drag out for ages without a full-time score. When at last William decided to pull his finger out and fight properly, he got a result, beating Louis' lads 'game, set and match' at La Hogue in 1697.

This long war had been financed by the brand new Bank of England who raised cash by issuing shares to anyone who wanted to invest in it at 8% interest. This created the first National Debt which I believe we're still paying back (maybe because we keep borrowing from it!). Another great first was William's idea. He discovered it was much easier to fight a war if you have a group of guys from only one party. They were called a Cabinet and met in secret which they still do.

1700 – War with France No. 2

Those damn French never learn and the eighteenth century opened with another war brewing. This time things looked a little more tricky. Louis XIV's grandson had taken over as King of Spain in 1700 which gave France control of the Spanish Empire and James II's young son, James III (still in France) was recognised (if only by the Frogs) as King of England when his dad died in 1702.

Much worse than this, our much loved Queen Mary died trying out an exciting new disease called smallpox. 'Orange Billy', not to be outdone, died a few years later making a mountain out of a molehill when his clumsy horse tripped over one.

Meanwhile

1630 – First public advertising was seen in France. (Perrier? Neau!).

1635 – First tobacco sold in France was on a doctor's prescription. Trust the French to get things round the wrong way.

1637 – The first umbrella kept a Frenchman dry.

1642 – Income and property tax introduced in England.

1650 – World population reached 500 million.

1652 – Tea first drunk in Britain. When it was sold to the public, eight years' later, priests and writers were outraged claiming the strange brown drink was dangerous to health, morals and public order (which of course it is).

1662 – The Royal Society for Improving Natural Knowledge was started by Christopher Wren (the church chap), John Evelyn (the writer chap), Robert Boyle (the scientist chap) and Isaac Newton (the apple chap). The age of science was on the starting blocks and superstition was on the way out.

1666 – At last! The first Cheddar cheese.

1666 – Stradivari made best violin ever seen (or heard).

1667 – French army chucked the first hand grenades.

1675 – Paris became the centre of European culture.

1680 – The last Dodo die-died!

1698 – Tax on beards in Russia (only on men).

Chapter 24

Great Britain vs France – The Final

Mary's sister, Anne, was catapulted into power in 1702 aged thirty-eight. Although dull and lethargic herself she was ace at employing chaps who weren't. Best of all was a young soldier called John Churchill (watch out for that name). His official title was Duke of Marlborough. This name should have carried a French government health warning as he was determined to shut the pesky French up for good. He thought sieges were a bit soppy and decided to have a proper fight. So started the war of the Spanish Succession. Britain's main plan was to help put an Austrian prince on the throne of Spain instead of a French one. It seems like the Spanish princes didn't get a look in.

1704 – War with France No. 3

Marlborough and his army apparently marched straight up the Rhine to the Danube (bet they had wet socks) and joined our mates the Austrians. At the battle of Blenheim, this terrible team crushed the combined French and Bavarian army. This was the beginning of the end for Louis who asked nicely if he could make a pact with us (creep). The Tories in England were all for it, but it was just sour grapes because their opponents, the Whigs, were making cash out of the war. Marlborough pressed on and took Gibralta which pleased Anne so much she built, paid for and gave him Blenheim Palace, a socking great house north of Oxford.

'See, Sir, here's the grand approach,
This way is for his Grace's coach . . .
The Council chamber's for debate,
And all the rest are rooms of state.'
'Thanks, Sir,' I cried, ''tis very fine,
But where d'ye sleep and where d'ye dine?
I find by all you have been telling,
That 'tis a house but not a dwelling.'

Pope . . . (not THE Pope)

1707 – Great Britain

Meanwhile, back at the war, Marlborough drove the French out of the Netherlands and the good old Austrians chased them out of Italy. Louis begged for peace but the Whigs, who were having a ball, made an act of Union with Scotland instead, and in 1707 we became GREAT Britain for the first time. Someone called Jack designed a rather gaudy flag and rather cockily named it after himself.

Crazed with success, the British went on to capture Minorca (big deal!), Nova Scotia in Canada and Newfoundland – which, by then, had been 'found' for a couple of hundred years. By this time poor Louis was positively grovelling for a treaty (yeah – he would, wouldn't he?).

1713 – Treaty of Utrecht

The Tories were by this time much more powerful than the Whigs, who were tottering. Being spoilsports they decided to call Marlborough in from abroad. Great Britain then signed the Treaty of Utrecht with France, and Britain and Austria divvied up the spoils. The Tories then set about destroying the Whig party, even though it seems their party was well and truly over.

Anne was absolutely whacked out having given birth to 15 children all of which unfortunately died. History says she died in

1714 of lethargy (having 15 kids can hardly be called lethargic!), leaving no heirs.

By the Way

Britannia, that funny woman we used to see on the back of old pennies, often confuses people. There she is, looking like a Roman, sitting in what looks like an amphibious wheelchair and draped in the Union Jack – which can't have existed. Don't worry, she's a fictional character representing Britain as a woman.

She first appeared on a golden Roman coin in AD 161 (without the flag), and later in 1665 on a copper coin (what a come-down). The model for Britannia was Frances Stuart, Duchess of Richmond – as if you didn't know.

Chapter 25:

German George 1714

In the last 700 years England had been ruled by Danish, Norman, French, Welsh, Scottish and Dutch sovereigns. The new Great British were still surprised, however, when an old, fat, non-English speaking German showed up to be their king. George I, a

Hanoverian, arrived in London in 1714 having tidily imprisoned his wife, Sophia, for life. He'd spent much of his early life devoted to 'vine, vimmin and song' and didn't stop when he got here. He was terribly unpopular so we'll say no more about him, save he ruled for thirteen years and died in 1727.

1715 – Old Pretender

Soon after he arrived there was a Jacobite rebellion known as the '15, mostly supported by all the Scots uptight with England's newish Union with Scotland. They wanted James Francis Edward, Chevalier de St George, Prince of Wales (hope you've got all that) to be James III of England. He was known as the Old Pretender presumably because he had spent most of his life in France pretending to be a king. His rebellion only lasted six weeks, after which he sailed home feeling rather stupid. The trouble was that most people were far more interested in trying to make an honest (or dishonest) buck or two gambling on trade with the tropics, than in worrying who was king.

1720 – South Sea Bubble

The most famous outfit was the South Sea Company which everyone invested in. Unfortunately it grew out of all proportion through speculation until the 'Bubble' burst and everyone lost not only their shirts, but their trousers as well.

The first proper Prime Minister was then invented and called Sir Robert Walpole. His job was to clear up the mess and keep the country on an even keel under Whig rule.

Chapter 26

George's Boy George

If George I was not much to write home about, his son Prince George was no better. His dad thought he was a rude little oik and chucked him out of the court (sounds a bit like some of our tennis players). The bolshy young prince promptly set up his own court round the corner, and became a real thorn in his father's side. Being totally ignorant in science, literature and reasonable personal habits, history would probably have preferred to forget about him. His reign, however, was to be chock-full of new exciting things albeit no thanks to him.

1727 – George II

Old George, his dad, died suddenly in 1727 on holiday in Holland, and the prince was crowned before the old man was cold. As well as

all his other shortcomings, he was a cocky devil by all accounts and although on the short side would strut and pose when given half a chance. He was no wimp, however, and it should be noted that he was the last British sovereign to lead an army in battle.

1739 – Another War

Walpole was forced into a nice little war with Spain which soon got out of hand to such an extent that we were soon mixing it with just about everyone. Walpole soon discovered that although OK as a domestic Prime Minister he was not much cop at wars. He was swiftly replaced by a chap named Henry Pelham, who, with his fearfully corrupt brother, the Duke of Newcastle, managed to string the war out for eight years, settling nothing. All it did manage to achieve was a unique opportunity for another Jacobite rebellion called the '45.

1745 – The Great Pretender
This took place when another Stuart pretender to our throne, Prince Charlie, (known rather 'camply' as Bonnie) landed in Scotland with seven of his mates to stir up the heavy Highlanders again (as they'd all had a nice rest). Being a good looking, smooth talker, Charles soon had them all behind him and promptly took Edinburgh. They then went on to pan the English under general 'Johnnie' Cope at Prestonpans in 1745. Fortunately the English had their hands full with away matches so The Bonnie Prince thought the time was ripe to have a go down south again. All he needed was a little help from his old friends the French and a few thousand English volunteers that he'd been counting on from over the border. He waited and waited, but no one showed. Charlie, fed up with hanging around, set off south with 6,500 men. They got within 125 miles of London when they heard that loads of English soldiers had just arrived from Europe where they'd been defending Austria against France (busy business, soldiering!). Rather red-faced, they tiptoed back to Scotland with their sporrans between their legs.

1746 – Culloden
They thwarted the now-attacking English back at Falkirk but carelessly lost Edinburgh. The grand final was held at Culloden Moor in 1746. The English were led by William, Duke of Cumberland (later known as 'the Butcher'), who was the son of George II. It was a jolly fierce, nasty battle and, when the full-time whistle blew, there were a thousand dead Highlanders on the pitch. 'The Butcher' and his not-very-merry men rounded up the prisoners, survivors and injured and mercilessly 'kill-ted' them. The government in London then passed some neat laws to finish Highland clan life forever (what a McShame!). In gratitude the English named a flower 'the Sweet William' in the Duke's honour.

The Scots, rather ungraciously, renamed the Stinkwort weed 'Stinking Billy' as their mark of deep respect.

1748 – Redcoats

Charles, it seems, then made several movies in which he starred as the romantic fugitive, dodging round the highlands, seducing pretty maidens and avoiding the English patrols. These were called 'Redcoats' owing to their red coats. Centuries later, they appeared again – still as Redcoats – working in Butlin's holiday (or should I say prison) camps.

The Bonnie Prince caught the next French ship to Europe, where he ended up in Rome. He died forty years later – a hopeless drunk. When his brother gave up the ghost in 1807 the Stuarts had finally had it as far as the throne was concerned.

By the Way
George II was one of the loudest snorers in history (Abraham Lincoln was second).

By the Way (again)
All the weeping willows in England come from a Turkish basket of figs sent to Lady Suffolk in the early eighteenth century. Her chum, Alexander Pope, obviously not too struck on figs, planted a bit of the basket instead (that's poets for you) and this grew into the first weeping willow to be seen in this country.

Meanwhile
1705 – Halley predicted the return (in 1758) of his famous comet. The flaming thing keeps coming back.

1709 – Cristofori invented a piano, and probably could only play 'Chopsticks'.

1718 – Puckle patented the machine-gun enabling one to kill more people quicker.

1731 – 10 Downing Street built to put Prime Ministers in.

1752 – Benjamin Franklin invented the lightning conductor (no bus jokes please).

1754 – The Earl of Sandwich, a compulsive gambler, hated leaving the card table to get a meal. Instead he had a servant bring him some meat between two bits of bread and inadvertently invented – the ham roll!

Chapter 27

Meanwhile, Back In The Old Country – 1750

It's surprising to realise that the population was still only around 5,200,000. It wasn't that people didn't know how to make babies – with no birth control (rubber hadn't been invented), it was quite the opposite. Britain was such an unhealthy place, that if you reached forty you'd done pretty well. Infant mortality was horrendous and many of their poor mums died in or around childbirth as well. Added to this, no one knew that disease was associated with dirt and, oh boy were they dirty! All drinking and washing water came from the rivers (Perrier – where were you) and, having no lavs, guess what they threw in the rivers?

Beautiful Britain

Rubbish, if not eaten by our little furry friends, was left to rot in the streets, and they really ponged (the streets!). As water was so short the noble English still tended not to bathe that much. If you were rich you might wash your clothes once a month; if poor, you wouldn't bother. Consequently, diseases like smallpox, typhus and 'jail fever' were all the rage.

Mind you, the French were no better. There's a lovely ancient English insult that goes – if you want to hide something from a Frenchman, put it under a bar of soap!

Health

Doctors were not much use. Most of them had no qualifications at all, and had no more status than any other craftsmen. Housewives would rely on passed down herbal remedies, superstition, or apothecaries. These guys were a bit like homoeopaths now, selling mostly herbal pills, potions and ointments of their own invention. Whether these quacks did any real good either then or now is something that might be wiser not to go into. Barbers at that time were also dentists and surgeons on the side. Sounds all rather convenient. You could have a short back and sides, a tooth pulled, and your leg off, without leaving the chair. As anaesthetics hadn't been invented, you could choose a stiff drink or a bang on the head (anyone with any sense might just have had both).

Agriculture

Major changes happened in agriculture and therefore rural life in the eighteenth century (1700–1800). Up till then, if you'd gone up in your helicopter (which you probably wouldn't have had), you would have seen that the countryside looked a bit like a multi-coloured parquet floor, interrupted by little hamlets of a few ramshackle houses. Each villager would have several individual strips of land. The daft thing was that these ruddy strips weren't next to each other, so he'd often have to trudge long distances between them. Each village would have a largish area called the common land on which the common man could graze his common animals.

Enclosure Acts

The Enclosure Acts were invented to sort this nonsense out. Basically, a couple of guys called commissioners would pitch up at your village once an Enclosure Act had been passed on it. They would then take all the land from everyone and share it out again. The theory was that all the little bits would be lumped together into bigger bits that would be much easier to farm. The poorer you were, however, the more you got screwed on the deal, losing your rights to the much depleted common land to boot. The squires, rich farmers and the local parson (for whom the Lord provided extremely well) usually cleaned up. The country began to look much as it does now with large fields, or enclosures, hemmed in by hedges.

Also the rotation system of farming became all the rage at this time. A farmer would divide his land in, say, four bits and grow different things in each leaving one to lie fallow and just grow grass. Each year he'd swap them round.

Chapter 28:

The Great Land Grab! – 1750

After the war with France, and Bonnie Prince Charlie's abortive rebellion, there were a few rather nervous years of peace. Both Britain and France were scrabbling around, trying to nick land off poor unsuspecting natives all over the uncivilised world. At the same time they were both trying to curry favour (not flavour) with what was left of the great Mogul Empire in India. The French

managed to set up a load of froggy forts along the St Lawrence, Hudson, Ohio, and Mississippi rivers forcing the British colonies to stay along the coast.

By 1755 both sides really took their gloves off and decided to start the Seven Years War. The teams were Britain and Prussia versus France and Austria. The British started badly and were severely slaughtered in America.

1756 – Minorca Goes

The wars went from bad to worse until – shock, horror! England finally lost Minorca (again). This, of course, called for the most drastic action. Luckily a chap called William Pitt the Elder (elder than who? you might ask) joined the government. With the help of General Wolfe – who huffed and puffed and blew the French down – he got back India and Canada. It was called The Year of Victories and by the time the French put their hands up and signed the Peace of Paris in 1763 all they had left were two measly trading stations somewhere in India. Poor old George II missed the party, however, having died of a heart attack, aged seventy-seven, a couple of years before.

By the Way

When things were all going wrong up India way, a complete British garrison of 146 men were captured by the Nawab of Bengal and put in what came to be known as the 'Black Hole of Calcutta'. This was a windowless, ventilationless chamber only 20 ft square. It occurred on the night of 21st June 1756 and when the guards brought them their Cornflakes the following morning, only 23 had survived (which is why they *didn't* get in the Guinness Book of Records).

Chapter 29:

Tea Time!

In 1760 George II had been succeeded by – wait for it – George III who was far worse than his dad or grandad. He wanted to wear his crown every day and rule properly like the olden days, not having to listen to any soppy old Cabinet. This spelt the end for the Whigs who'd been sitting pretty for more than fifty years. It was time for the king and the 'king's friends' to have a go. The king's best friend and adviser was Lord 'Scotch' Bute. The London mobs hated Bute and the king, who they thought was a mummy's boy, so they burned boots (a bad pun on Bute) and petticoats (to represent George's mum) in a huge bonfire.

Pitt was dismissed, having long been regarded as a megalomaniac, but without his leadership, government after government failed. Relations with the colonies became frosty, to say the least, mainly because they refused to tax themselves and send the cash home. It was a bit like asking someone to beat themselves with their own stick, but the government reckoned they knew best. In the end Parliament decided to do the taxing which steamed up the colonies even more. This row was to lead, eventually, to the American War of Independence.

1773 – Boston Tea Party

The king had hired a real crawler, Lord North, to keep Parliament quiet. He carried on mismanaging affairs of state – especially in America. Although lots of these taxes were repealed a huge tax on tea remained. The result was a huge fancy dress party in Boston when the drunken colonists, dressed as Red Indians, invented a vast, rather salty beverage by throwing £18,000 pounds worth of the East India Company's finest tea into the harbour.

George, who was thought to be going crazy, tried to make it up with Pitt, making him the Earl of Chatham. Pitt, though quite chuffed to be 'lorded' was still, unfortunately, totally opposed to government policy, as were the regenerated Whig party. It was all too late, however, for on the 4th July 1776 Congress issued a Declaration of Independence making George Washington their first President. To this day, Americans have a party, set off fireworks and light bonfires on Independence Day to celebrate breaking away from us lot. Luckily (maybe), Canada remained loyal along with a few of the middle American colonies. Britain occupied New York in an attempt to separate New England from the southern states, but our general (and, believe it or not, comedy playwright) Burgoyne, having advanced from Montreal, was forced to surrender at Saratoga to the revolting Yanks.

1777 – War with France No. 4

The sneaky French and Spanish, never ones to miss a chance of having a go at their oldest foe – the British – decided to make out they were real champions of American liberty and declared war on us. In 1780 the Dutch joined them, followed by just about everyone else. Even Ireland joined in and a 10,000 strong mob, led by the loony Lord George Gordon, took over London for four days. The uprising, famous for its widespread murder and destruction, was called the 'No Popery Riot'. For some idea of what it must have been like, stand outside the Goat and Shamrock at closing time on any Friday night! Lord Gordon (son of Cosmo Gordon) was famous for being totally eccentric. He libelled just about everyone including the French Ambassador, Marie Antoinette, and then the Queen of France. Personally I can't see what all the fuss was about, seeing as we hated the darned French anyway. In 1788 poor Lord Gordon was chucked into Newgate, a particularly horrid prison founded by Sir Dick Wittington, where he languished for the rest of his days. Mind you he was lucky! Many of the rioters were executed on a brilliant new 'Hanging Machine' (or gallows) which remained in Britain until relatively recently.

1782 – Peace Again

Our 'War Against Just About Everybody' had ended, and Britain was for once trying to keep on the right side of everyone. George III had managed to lose most of our new Empire except for India, Canada and Gibralta (which seems plenty to me).

If you ever wondered why our Queen doesn't have more say in modern Britain, you can blame old George. After his constant bungling the Crown was never allowed to poke its nose into the country's affairs again. The Cabinet was restored, with a Prime Minister who was head of the majority party in the Commons – just like now. George did, nevertheless, prefer the Tories to the Whigs and asked young William Pitt the Younger (old William Pitt the Elder's younger boy) to form a ministry. He was only twenty-four.

Mechanisation

Things were zipping along really fast in Britain by this time. Funny-looking, and slightly crude, machines and tools were constantly appearing in the country, helping farmers become more efficient. The beginning of mechanisation in industry meant that

103

the rich were becoming richer and the poor much, much poorer. Never had the country been so obviously divided, and the natives were getting restless. The dear old Whigs who were all for reform were not to get a look in for fifty years. The Tories, on the other hand, were far too concerned squeezing cash out of the colonies to really lose any sleep over what was happening in Britain.

1789 – French Revolution

Everyone fell about laughing in Britain when they heard about the French Revolution. Watching your old enemy tearing itself apart is always nice from a safe distance. When they topped their King and Queen, however, and started attacking anyone in authority, the

smiles disappeared and the Tories realised that the same thing could happen here if they weren't extremely careful. Strangely enough, old George III was quite liked over here. In spite of everything, the British have never really gone in for Royalty bashing.

1792 – Censorship

The Tories weren't taking any risks, however, and banned the cheaper press. They wouldn't have had to worry if it was these days – our cheap newspapers don't have any news – unless you count what topless Debbie's up to on 'Page Three'.

Public meetings were forbidden and the Act of Habeas Corpus was suspended. This meant that they could shove anyone they liked behind bars or down under to Australia without trial. Young William Pitt, I must explain, had decided – as soon as our Cook discovered Australia in 1770 – that it would be a great place to send all our convicts (who now own the country, and half the world's lager!).

Chapter 30

Napoleon Rules OK

Things were really hotting up in 'Gay Paree' with heads rolling from left, right and centre. Tumbrils (nice little wooden carts) carrying the poor nobility to – and their slightly shortened bodies from – Madame Guillotine, were as common as red buses in London.

This rough, tough way of setting up a Republic upset the rest of Europe, and soon France was at war with most of it – and doing surprisingly well. This was largely due to a funny 'petit homme' called Napoleon Bonaparte, commander of the new Republican army. This brilliant little fighter was soon to become Emperor of France in 1804 – and just about everywhere else. He was supposed to have had one of the highest IQ's ever recorded and only needed three to four hours sleep a night.

1800 – Britain Gets Nervous
You can imagine how jittery the Brits were getting by this time. Pitt realised that it was just a matter of time before those dratted

French looked over their shoulders and spotted their oldest enemy – us! He tried to do a deal with the Irish, combining the English and Irish Parliaments. This was no doubt because, in the past, the French had always used Ireland as a base from which to attack Britain. This drove poor, old, dopey George even further round the bend as he wouldn't have Catholics in the house, and flatly refused to have anything to do with it.

1801 – United Kingdom

After loads of cash went into the back pockets of the right people, this Anglo/Irish Union went through, and we became the United Kingdom. There was so much fuss, however, that Pitt resigned, and the strain of losing finally sent poor George completely crackers. He spent his last years wandering aimlessly through the huge empty

corridors of Windsor Castle, blind as a bat, deaf as a post, mad as a hatter and gibbering to himself. His white hair and beard hung nearly to his knees and he only ever wore an old purple dressing-gown. During these last years of his reign Britain was effectively ruled by the Dreadful Prince Regent (crowned George IV) but more of him later.

By the Way

It was around this time that William Brodie, a cabinetmaker, head of his union and member of the Edinburgh town council, became the subject of Robert Louis Stevenson's *The Strange Case of Dr Jekyll and Mr Hyde*. During the day he was a well-respected businessman but at night he led a gang of masked robbers. Both of 'him' were eventually caught and hanged.

Meanwhile

1760 – Kew Gardens opened.

1765 – A thirty-eight mile ditch was dug, filled with water, and called the Bridgewater Canal. Canals were soon to become real competitors to roads.

1766 – Cavendish discovered hydrogen to be lighter than air.

1769 – Arkwright invented the first water-powered spinning machine.

1774 – Joseph Priestley discovers dephlogisticated air. This was such a mouthful that they later, sensibly, called it oxygen.

1775 – James Watt uses a lot of this new oxygen up, fiddling around with his new-fangled steam engine.

1780 – The first fountain pen invented. Good for writers, and even better for geese (quills?).

1781 – The word QUIZ appears. A Dubliner named Daley bet he could introduce a new word into the English language. He chalked this strange word all over the city (first graffiti?) and everyone tried to guess what it meant. 'Quiz' was born – and its meaning obvious.

1783 – The Montgolfier brothers blew up a balloon, tied it to a basket, and flew away. They weren't the first, however, as earlier that year a sheep, a duck, and a cock had done the same thing watched by King Louis XVI and Marie Antoinette.

1785 – *The Times* newspaper appears for the first time.

1790 – Turner painted the first pictures that looked a bit the same either way up.

1795–1821 – John Keats wrote a lot of new poems which included Ode to a Nightingale and Ode to a Grecian Urn (please don't ask how much a Grecian earns). He should have got the poet's prize for the silliest girl-friend's name – Fanny Brawne!

Chapter 31:

Boney Gets The Boot

Pitt got it all wrong about Napoleon invading Ireland. Boney had a much more ambitious plan. Never one to do things by half, he planned to invade England by sea, air and would you believe it – tunnel. The air attack was going to be from huge, extremely dangerous looking troop-carrying balloons. The tunnel, planned in 1803, was supposed to pop up somewhere on our south coast and surprise us all. It's taken another 200 years to surprise us!!

1804 – War with France No. 5

Before Boney's boys had a chance to put the first spade into the French turf the whole business was scuppered by our very best sailor ever – Horatio Nelson. Although managing to lose things like his eye and his arm, and the contents of his stomach on each voyage he was no slouch when it came to sea battles. He first upset Boney, who was boss in Egypt, when he sank lots of his galleons in the Nile.

1805 – Battle of Trafalgar

Napoleon then thought of this great ruse. While the British fleet under Nelson was protecting the West Indies (which was like Britain's huge piggy bank) the French fleet would suddenly about turn and rush back to hit the unprotected British Isles. One day Nelson turned round and noticed – with his one good eye – that the French had gone, and quickly followed. The French fleet under Villeneuve unexpectedly met another British fleet under Admiral Calder coming from Britain, and was forced to Cadiz where they joined up with the Spanish fleet who were their mates. Nelson's ships caught up with Villeneuve and the Battle of Trafalgar began. By the end of the match the French and Spaniards had lost 4,400 men, with 2,500 wounded, and given 20,000 prisoners. Nelson only lost 450 men, with 1,200 injured, no ships and – oh yes – his life! His chums rather thoughtfully sent him home pickled in a barrel of navy brandy. Napoleon called it a day and gave up all hope of invading England. The Frogs I can safely say have never, to this day, forgiven us.

1808 – Revenge

Just to get his own back, however, Napoleon decided to blockade all British goods from the continental ports which he controlled (The Continental System). Silly little man! He'd obviously forgotten that although he ruled the land, we ruled the sea. The British thought – what's good for the goose is good for the gander. So we beat the French at their own game and stopped any of their goods going into these ports, effectively blockading them instead. This really got up the noses of the occupied continental countries who were getting more than a little fed up with this hook-nosed, red-haired French midget.

Meanwhile, back at the ranch, the Duke of Wellington was preparing an army to help the rebel Spanish nationalists, who'd had enough of French occupation. Wellington was a tough taskmaster, calling his lower ranks the 'scum of the earth'. He was none too impressed with his poncy officers either, who worried so much about their splendid, if somewhat sissy, uniforms, that they were often spotted taking umbrellas onto the battlefield so as not to get wet.

In 1813 Wellington dived into Europe and chased the French all over the place, finally catching and driving them out of Spain at Vittoria before crossing the Pyrenees.

1812 – Things Go Badly for Boney
Napoleon was having a rotten time invading Russia, partly because he had piles and could hardly ride his horse (not surprising); and

partly because when he finally reached Moscow everyone had cleared out apart from thieves and beggars. He'd lost 33,000 men getting there and on one day alone his senior surgeon had sawn off 200 shattered arms and legs (Frogs' legs?).

As they were leaving, the Ruskies set fire to their city and naughtily took all their fire engines. When the fire died down Napoleon realised how perishing cold Russia was and decided to get the first sleigh home. Unfortunately, it was cold enough to freeze the hind leg off a donkey so that his troops, who were fresh out of donkeys anyway, had to leg it (if they had any) home. Thousands died of exposure and starvation on the way back.

He fought on for another couple of years but by then the Russians had joined the Prussians and Austrians and were a formidable force. Meanwhile our boy Wellington was giving it plenty down in the South of France. The Russians captured Paris in 1814 so Bonaparte chucked in the towel.

The French decided they wanted a king again and little Boney was exiled to Elba, an island miles from anywhere.

Tired of beach life (strange for a Frenchman) Napoleon escaped back to France where Louis XVIII was enjoying being King for a bit.

1815 – Waterloo
The army – Boney was delighted to find – were still loyal to their funny ex-leader and followed him to the final showdown. This was the famous battle of Waterloo. Wellington started badly and nearly

got the boot (sorry), but at the last minute the Russians arrived – like the cavalry in a cowboy film – and Boney was defeated once and for all. So ended The 20 Years War.

When Britain came out of the war, she found that she'd got a better Empire than ever. She now had Canada, Australia (though full of convicts), India, the Cape Colonies, Ceylon and Guiana. Of course we still had the scattered islands of the West Indies, but they were turning out to be more trouble than they were worth.

1816 – Back in Britain
Despite all this new-found wealth and power it didn't do the average working man in Britain much good. They were just exploited by the nouveau rich and the aristocracy. It wasn't as if they could do anything about it, as they weren't even allowed to vote or have meetings. Despite this the population was rising – probably because there weren't so many dreadful catastrophes to carry them off.

1819 – Bad Times
This post war prosperity was short lived, however. It's all very well churning out loads of wonderful new products but if, after a war, nobody's got any francs, liras or pesetas to pay for them it's all a bit pointless. The Corn Laws weren't much help either. These taxes on imported wheat had been running for years to make the home-grown stuff competitive. The tax at this time was now so high, and

our wheat production so insufficient, that it meant that if you were broke, bread went off the menu. It must also be noted that, despite all the clever new diseases, the number of mouths that now had to be fed had risen to 7,000,000.

The Arts
Dr Johnson and Boswell, both famous writers, had formed the Literary Club – a right arty affair. Members included such all time greats as Oliver Goldsmith and Edmund Burke (fellow scribblers), Sir Joshua Reynolds and Thomas Gainsborough (good with the old paint brushes), Adam Smith (economist), Richard Sheridan (the playwright), Edward Gibbon (a serious historian!), and Robert Adam (builder of posh houses).

By the Way

When Napoleon died in 1821 his head was shaved and the individual hairs were given out as souvenirs. His heart was put into a silver vase and his stomach into a pepper pot. A bit of his intestines, which ended up at the Royal College of Surgeons, was destroyed in an air raid in 1940. More bizarre still, his most private part, said to be only an inch long and looking like a sea horse, was offered for sale at Christies, the auction house, in 1972. It was listed as a 'small dried up object' but unfortunately failed to reach the reserve price. Apparently the little thing had been nabbed by his confessor priest (I wonder what he'd told him!). Who's got it now?

Meanwhile
1802 – Dalton finally found the atom which was rather difficult owing to it being a bit on the small side.

1803 – Fulton invented the first steamboat and the first torpedo (to sink it).

1807 – Slave trade abolished throughout all the British colonies (about time too!).

1810 – Bikes invented. They weren't much cop, however, as they didn't have any pedals.

1812 – Britain's first cannery set up in Bermondsey, London. Tin cans had only just been invented. Strangely enough, they didn't invent a can opener for another fifty years. I bet I can guess your next question!

1814 – Wordsworth regarded as our top poet. He wrote a daft rhyme about daffs.

1815 – Proper roads started to appear, running the length and breadth of Britain, financed by tolls which were charged at turnpikes. It's interesting to note that after 175 years of free road travel, there's talk of bringing tolls back – (that's progress?).

1819 – A ten-year-old blind boy, Louis Braille invented – Braille.

1820 – Macadam invented tarmac for roads. This made life easier for stage and mail coaches to travel at night. This in turn made life even easier for highwaymen like Dick Turpin, who robbed the rich to pay . . . himself!

Chapter 32

Gorgeous George

Crazy old George III finally gave up the ghost in 1820 – not that anyone noticed – as did Castlereagh in 1822, one of his top ministers, who'd also gone wacko. Although Castlereagh's chums had managed to keep him away from sharp objects (there weren't that many ways of killing yourself in those days) he managed to find a tiny penknife and . . . you can imagine the rest.

The Prince Regent, now George IV, had been a right trial to his poor mum and dad all his life. He was a gambler, spendthrift, womaniser and incredible drinker. 'Drunk as a Lord' is an expression directly attributable to our George. Even before he got his dad's gold hat on he had become despised by the British commonfolk, so much so, that he was always surrounded by soldiers, who caught most of the stones intended for him.

Mrs Fitzherbert

He was a sneaky beggar as well. He'd secretly married a widow called Mrs Fitzherbert. It had to be secret because she was a Catholic and all hell would have broken loose if his folks had got to hear about it. As it was, however, it was one of the worst kept secrets ever and eventually our noble Prince dumped her callously, knowing it would put the kybosh on eventually being king. She must have got over it, however, as she is one of the only people to go down in history as having died of exhaustion from a fit of laughing.

Caroline of Brunswick

He quickly married Caroline of Brunswick who, although a German, was definitely born on the right side of the sheets and managed for once to have a legitimate kid. He didn't fancy her for very long (surprise, surprise) and deviously spread tacky rumours about her honour.

While she was on holiday abroad, he wrote and offered her £50,000 not to come home – which sounds rather reasonable to me. She wouldn't hear of it, however, and came back to much public acclaim. George then tried divorce and, using the government like a blunt instrument, attempted to get her for adultery. The magic combination of no evidence and immense public popularity, however, got the case kicked out even though a divorce had been OK'd by the Lords. George then prevented her being let into Westminster Abbey when they were both due to be crowned in 1821. This was the last straw and the shock led to her demise shortly after. George, true to form, went on to live with (and kick out) lots more women.

Someone famous once described him as 'a bad son, a bad husband, a bad father, a bad subject, a bad monarch, and a bad friend' (not bad eh!). Having said all this, however, someone else famous said of him – 'he was very polished . . . knew how to listen . . . was affectionate, sympathetic and gallant . . . with some wit and great penetration'. In fact, if you were his mate, most people thought he was a great laugh, terribly charming and extremely flash with his cash. His parties sounded really fab with no expense spared,

and it must be noted he was a recognised expert in food and wine. George was also extremely kind and supportive to artists and writers like Jane Austen and Walter Scott.

Unfortunately, his generosity didn't extend to his poorer subjects of whom he was, apparently, blissfully unaware. His extravagance was unequalled even though he was supposed to make do on what would now be £2,000,000 a year (Try me! Try me!). He built the rather gross Buckingham Palace as a little London pad, and the totally over the top (and brill) Brighton Pavilion for somewhere different to go at weekends.

1822 – Foreign Affairs
Meanwhile back to what was happening elsewhere. The king had long ceased favouring the Whigs, and a new Tory government was born under Lord Liverpool with three prominent liberal members –

Canning, Huskisson and Peel. Canning told the United States that Britain would help if any of those nasty European countries started any funny business. Huskisson repealed the Combination Acts which had made Trade Unions illegal. Peel invented the first proper police who were called 'Peelers' in 1829. Women (police) weren't thought of till 1920 but probably arrested anyone who referred to them by that name.

1829 – Catholics
Catholics for the first time (incredibly) since 1673 were allowed to have high position. This was OK until they tried to get into Parliament which the Tories thought was well over the top. However, faced with a civil war in Ireland, they passed the Catholic Emancipation Act in 1829. This split the Tories so much that, at the General Election, the year after George IV's succession, they lost to the wiley Whigs. The Tory stranglehold on Parliament went down the drain after sixty years of power.

Chapter 33

England Gets Into Training – 1830

Canals in England were becoming a bit of a liability. In hot weather they tended to dry up and in cold weather they froze. If this wasn't bad enough, the owners were beginning to get a bit greedy, charging pocketfuls of cash (as tolls), if you wanted to use them. The answer came with the invention of the steam locomotive. The first proper modern railway came in 1825 and ran between Stockton and Darlington. Five years later the famous Liverpool–Manchester line opened. This was largely due to George Stephenson who not only won a competition to build the best engine, but also made and laid the rails for it to run on.

Rail Travel

The good old class system was not forgotten. The rich travelled first class in comfortable enclosed carriages. The not-so-rich were seated, but travelled in the open air. The other poor souls travelled

in open trucks, like cattle, with no seats (not that cattle would necessarily want them). All this would have been fine if the track ran along the sunny Côte d'Azur, but Liverpool to Manchester – please!

The Rocket, as it was called, reached unheard of speeds of up to – wait for it – 29 mph. This really brassed off the folk whose homes and land lay alongside the new tracks. They claimed it would lead to no birds or horses (God knows why?), eggless hens, milkless cows, and general mayhem. Moan, moan, moan!! They should have seen our M25 . . . on a *good* day!

1830 – Huskisson Gets the Rocket

At the opening ceremony Huskisson, the ex-Cabinet minister, largely responsible for the building of the railway, had rather a horrid accident. He got out of his carriage while the Rocket was turning round and was gaily rabbiting with the Duke of Wellington. While being congratulated, someone yelled to him to get out of the way. Poor Huskisson panicked and leapt back straight in front of the brand new engine which ran over his legs (ouch). He died shortly afterwards (and probably didn't get his fare back).

Coaches

The Stagecoach companies soon went broke as tracks criss-crossed the land like the lines on the palm of your hand, but in the towns it was a different story. Steam coaches were becoming all the rage until boring old Parliament passed a boring old law that said they couldn't travel at more than 2 mph. Even then they had to have

some poor nerd walking sixty yards ahead carrying a red flag. I know some people that drive as if that law's still in force. Anyway steam coaches soon dropped out and horse-drawn coaches stayed (and messed up the streets) for many more years.

In the early nineteenth century only one person in a hundred had a vote and some newish cities like Manchester and Birmingham weren't represented in Parliament at all. The old Iron Duke (Wellington) thought this was fine and strongly disapproved of doing anything about it. Around this time (1820), revolution hung heavy in the air all over Europe. In England, the Enclosure Movement had forced loads of little farmers into the red and they were sucked into the towns where all the horrible smoke-belching factories were spreading like weeds on a back lawn.

By the Way

As Mrs Fitzherbert couldn't be seen in public with the Prince Regent, he had a tunnel dug between his flash Pavilion and her place, across the road.

Working Conditions

As supply was greater by far than demand, the unscrupulous owners only employed those who'd work for the least money (what's different!), so wages actually shrank. Whole families, including little kids, had to work long hours just to get enough to eat. If they got sick it was tough bananas as far as the factory owners were concerned. They were as happy as pigs in muck, living in huge country houses, not giving a damn about the conditions their workers were forced to suffer. Trade Unions took years before they had enough clout to tell these rich skinflints where to get off.

The natives were getting restless, however, and there were strikes and mini-riots all over the shop. The Whigs, who didn't have the same blinkered view as the Tories, realised that they'd better do something. Led by Earl Grey (of smelly tea fame) they managed to squeeze a Reform Bill through which started to sort things out.

The Reforms of this Era

1. To get rid of all the pocket or 'rotten' Boroughs which sometimes had carried as many votes as huge towns.
2. £20,000 a year was to be given to church societies who were educating young children (presumably not the poor miserable little perishers that were working).
3. The State assumed responsibility for the poor. They didn't do much, but they did assume responsibility!

4. The Municipal Reform Act. This meant that towns had to mind their own business through municipalities elected by the rate-payers.
5. The Factories Act was passed. This meant that kids of under nine shouldn't work and that when they did, it shouldn't be for more than nine hours. This was all very well, but it doesn't take the Brain of Britain to fathom out that they weren't working for fun, and that if they didn't, the family would be in a worse state than before.
6. The Poor Law Amendment Act was passed in 1834. Groups of parishes clubbed together to form Poor Law Unions with an elected board of governors. The net result of this turned out to be the infamous workhouses where, if you were a pauper and having a miserable time, you went there and had a worse one. They were, therefore, mostly full of widows and orphans who had little choice.

Chapter 34

Just William

As far as monarchs were concerned, we'd had weak ones, strong ones, jolly ones, wicked ones, grumpy ones and gay ones but George IV had been the pits. The Crown had never reached such an all time low. When he died, the next one up was William, his brother. George's daughter, Charlotte, who would have been queen, had selfishly died in 1817. When William first heard of her death he realised that soon he would be king as old George already had one foot in the grave. At the time he was living with his housekeeper who looked after him (in more ways than one) and had given him several children. William realised she wouldn't do and that her time was up. He quickly changed her for a better model, marrying instead Princess Adelaide of Saxe-Meiningen who, although a bit of a dragon, had far more Crown 'cred'.

Country Couple
William IV had always been a bit of a sailor having started on ships at fourteen. He'd become a close chum of Horatio Nelson and was given the actual bullet which killed him, to treasure for ever (sick or what?). He hated cities, so when he married his Fraulein, they went to live in Windsor which in those days was all fields. Adelaide spent most of her time running a model dairy (you'd think he could have bought her a real one).

William was a bit of an old fusspot by all accounts – faddy, snappy, often grouchy, always getting uptight over the silliest things, and constantly repeating himself... repeating himself. Mind you the poor old beggar, who was in his sixties, had a right to be a bit fed up. When he succeeded to the throne in 1830 he discovered he'd been left mounds of paperwork to do, owing to the mess his brother had left things in. It's reported that he had to dip his hands in a bowl of hot water regularly because the constant signing of documents caused agony to his rheumatic joints.

1835 – More Reforms

William's reign, though short, saw momentous changes. He had eventually consented to the Reform Bills. Big deal! If he hadn't there'd have been a civil war. These bills, in retrospect, went a long way towards the process of government 'of the people, by the people, for the people' which we now call democracy. We might not have it – but at least we know what to call it!

At this time a whole new sort of people were emerging, neither particularly rich nor particularly poor. They were to grow into the dreaded Great British Middle Class.

On a lighter note, William was the first monarch to let Londoners stroll about in (and mess up) his huge back gardens which are now the Royal Parks.

Adelaide, his gripey and somewhat haughty wife, had a thing about kids (as both hers had died) and was always having loads of nephews and nieces round to their castle for tea. There was, however, one little girl who didn't get invited, as her mum, the Duchess of Kent, couldn't stand the Queen. She was a rather plain, strange and very serious kid who always played alone. She was to become the smallest but longest reigning monarch that Britain ever had.

Chapter 35

V For Victoria

When only eleven Princess Victoria was told that one day she'd be Queen. She wasn't too wild about it at first and bawled her eyes out. When she had stopped snivelling, she sat bolt upright and swore to her governess, 'I'll be good'.

She was crowned when eighteen in 1837, a funny-looking little thing (five foot), with pop eyes and a tiny little cupid's-bow mouth. She wore sombre clothes from the word go and didn't seem to get the jokes much. She was guided by the Prime Minister, Lord Melbourne, who told her to take it easy at first and not rock any boats. She managed to keep her funny wee nose out of public affairs for a couple of years, but when Melbourne resigned due to his position being so weak, she had a real scrap with his successor, Sir Robert Peel. He'd told her that she must replace her Ladies of the Bedchamber who were Whigs – with Tories. She refused – Peel resigned – Melbourne came back – she said sorry to Peel – and everyone lived happily ever after.

1838 – Prince Albert

Well! not actually 'ever' after, I must confess. When approaching marriage, two years later in 1840, Melbourne gradually lost his influence with her and old Peely got in again. The object of Victoria's affection was Prince Albert of Saxe-Coburg, her cousin, who she'd quietly fancied for years. It beats me why they always seemed to marry Germans (fat lot of good it ever did us). It's interesting to note; because she was a queen and he was only a prince, she had to do the asking. All they really had to do to keep the support of the nation was to stay married and have loads of nice normal nippers. Court life, as you now know, had been a bit dicky for many years to say the very least. After all, the young couple followed a bad king (George II), a mad king (George III), and a total buffoon (George IV).

1840 – Hungry 40s

The years between 1840 and 1850 were called the 'hungry 40s'. This was because 1. wages were terribly low, and 2. the Corn Laws were still keeping bread prices terribly high. A loaf of bread cost almost as much as some poor devil's daily wage. When the potato crop failed in 1845, thousands of Irish died of starvation and the rest went to America where they all seemed to become slightly soppy policemen in films! Victoria wrote in her diary that the Irish famine was 'too terrible to think of' so – apart from cutting down on an extra slice of toast for breakfast – she didn't.

Things only cheered up when Sir Robert Peel, who'd taken over from Melbourne, chucked the Corn Laws in favour of free trade, bringing bread prices down instantly. Despite this Victoria still thought he was a creep, but realised that being the head of the Conservative (new name for Tory) party she had to either like it or lump it. Vicky therefore decided to like it and they eventually became quite matey.

1842 – Chartists

Britain wasn't alone with its widespread poverty. All over Europe the poor were on the verge of starving and revolution was again in the air. The growth in England of the middle classes and their representation in Parliament had really put the working classes' noses out of joint and they were feeling well fed up. A 'Charter' was prepared by six tame MPs and six workers, which again proposed 'Votes for All'. A monster petition was collected but, when Parliament predictably kicked it out, the only solution the 'Chartists' saw was to have a major punch up. 20,000 special constables were enrolled (including, believe it or not, the future Emperor Napoleon III) to meet a huge demonstration on Clapham Common, but in the end it rained cats and dogs and was a washout. Napoleon Junior, by the way, had crossed the channel with his Madame because his angry subjects were polishing up, and looking lovingly at, their dear old guillotine again.

1851 – The Great Exhibition

The British, as always, remained loyal and things started to cheer up a bit. Prince Albert organised 'The Great Exhibition' in Hyde Park which chuffed Victoria no end. A ginormous palace of glass and steel was erected and the British goods that we were trying to flog to punters from all over the world were displayed. If you can imagine a huge Ideal Home Exhibition – don't! It was actually quite tasteful. Victoria, unlike many of the Royals today, wasn't a snob

and preferred the simple life and simple folk of the country rather than knocking around with the fashion conscious trendies of London. She was happiest spending time with the old man and their nine kids either on the Isle of Wight or up in Scotland.

Albert the Diplomat

Prince Albert was gradually let in on all the affairs of State and turned out to be rather sensible. It was largely due to his intervention, that we didn't fall headlong into another war. A dispatch was about to be sent to the United States Government which was apparently so stroppy that there was only one way for them to react. Albert intervened, deleted the nasty bits, and saved our bacon. He was only forty-two at the time but, physically, seemed to have just about everything wrong with him. He died in the same year and Victoria never got over it. She built a daft memorial, a big bridge and a round hall; all are still to be seen in London and all are called Albert.

Poor Victoria put on a black dress and stayed indoors for over two years. She dealt with all the affairs of State from Buck House and when either the Liberals (new name for Whigs) or the Conservatives (new name for the Tories) wanted to see her, they had to go to the tradesmen's entrance. She was hardly to show her face (or black body) again till the 50th anniversary of her reign in 1887. The crowd went barmy as she was still, strangely enough, really popular. The lesson to all monarchs must be – if you want to stay on the right side of us common folk, keep your head down and don't give us anything to bitch about.

Chapter 36:

Any More For More War!

Politically loads had been happening. When old Peel died both the Conservative and the Liberal parties were split, neither managing to get a majority. The first coalition government was therefore formed under Lord Aberdeen with Palmerston in charge of wars. In 1854 we joined the French (Mon Dieu! Can you believe it?) to fight the Russians who were giving the Turks a hard time up the Crimea, an area by the Black Sea grabbed by the Ruskies in 1783.

1854 – Crimean War

It was a particularly nasty scrap conducted in the nastiest of conditions. Although the allies were winning, the cost was terrible. Thousands of our boys, on one occasion, found out the hard way when the stupid Lord Cardigan, commander of the Light Brigade, decided to see whether swords and bayonets could beat cannonballs at the Battle of Balaclava. The boys that weren't massacred suffered dreadfully from lack of food, and the freezing cold. Even the horses died from exposure (aah!). As if that wasn't enough, cholera came along and the death rate topped 100 a day.

Palmerston was made Prime Minister and stopped all the mucking about – winning the war in 1856.

1854 – Florence Nightingale

About the only person to come out of the whole thing with any credit, was Florence Nightingale who did wonders when she finally arrived at the military hospitals. Her actions inspired a whole new breed of women called Suffragettes who believed that they should have more say in how things were run and were to give the chauvinist politicians a great run for their money. Strange as it may seem, Florence was a terrible hypochondriac. When she got home from the war she went straight to bed telling everyone she had a terrible heart condition and that her life hung by a thread. It must

have been a blooming strong thread as she stayed tucked up for another fifty-four years before eventually being proved right (aged ninety).

1857 – Indian Mutiny
The Crimean war was neatly followed by the Indian Mutiny. It appears the Indians were getting their turbans in a twist over the non-too-subtle introduction of western ways. Apparently, it came to a head when they discovered that their soldiers were being supplied with cartridges greased in the fat of the sacred cow or the abominable pig. They went crazy. (I doubt if the cows or pigs were that wild about it either!) We quietened them down, however, and by 1858 the British government had India safely under its rather expensive boot.

1861 – American Civil War
This bloody war was an attempt by the southern states to break away from those of the north. It curiously pointed out the rift in thinking between the British rich and poor. Despite a cotton famine the working classes supported honest Abe Lincoln and the north, while the upper classes predictably favoured the rich southern slave owners. Parliament sensibly (for once) sat on the political fence and left them to it. When Lincoln and the north won, however, Britain's relations remained somewhat cool.

1864 – Bismarck

Palmerston's last attempt at diplomacy finally landed him in the sh . . . ade! Bismarck, head Prussian minister, wanted to grab two nice fat Austrian Duchies to add to his Empire. Palmerston jumped up and down and threatened him with God knows what. Bismarck went ahead – Palmerston did nothing – Bismarck triumphed – Palmerston died – and a tough new European power was born.

In 1871 the French Empire was eventually crushed by the Prussians (tee hee!) and we got their ex-Emperor (and ex-policeman) back, with his flash Spanish wife, Eugenie. Actually we shouldn't laugh because although we'd never been that pally with the French, it was certainly a case of better the Frog you know than the Kraut you don't. This, you see, really was the beginning of the German Empire and we all know what fun they were going to be.

Britain again remained neutral – not really surprising seeing as the Germans had married half our Royal family. In fact one of Victoria's girls was the wife of the new German Emperor himself. Had Victoria not been thick with Mr and Mrs Napoleon, who for some strange reason settled in Chislehurst, Britain might have got hitched to Germany (urghh – I hate sauerkraut).

Mind you Britain's Empire wasn't doing badly either during Victoria's reign. Our Empire's population expanded from 96 to 240 million people and the land it covered went from eight to twelve million square miles. You don't have to be Einstein to work out that one day there'd be a population problem.

By the Way

It is generally believed to be true that William Mildin the 14th Earl of Streatham was the inspiration for Edgar Rice Burroughs' *Tarzan of the Apes*. In 1868 he was reputedly shipwrecked on the West African coast when only eleven years old. He lived with a nice family of monkeys for fifteen years before being found and returned home (where he no doubt lived up a tree in the back garden).

Meanwhile

1827 – John Walker of Stockton-on-Tees invented matches and sells the first box.

1834 – Houses of Parliament burnt down (probably lit by a match). To be rebuilt as they are now.

1837 – Stocks banned. Stocks were a punishment used widely throughout Britain. The victim's arms and legs would be sandwiched between two heavy blocks of wood and he'd be left in a public place to be ridiculed by the hoi-polloi.

1837 – Charles Dickens wrote *Oliver Twist*.

1845 – Robert Thomson patented a hollow rubber tyre filled with horsehair (nice to know horses were still useful).

1848 – The Pre-Raphaelites started trying (rather badly) to paint pictures like early Italians.

1848 – Public Health Act passed to try to prepare for cholera which was on its way from all those foreigners.

1850s – Tennyson and Browning dominated poetry.

1853 – Press gangs were banned. These were gangs of savage sailors who grabbed ordinary men in the streets and forced them to be in the Navy.

1853–1856 – Livingstone crossed Africa (and got lost).

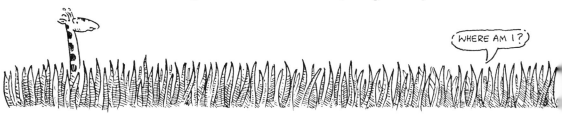

1856 – Bessemer mass-produced steel.

1858 – Brunel's 32,000 ton ship the *Great Eastern* launched in London. It was the biggest ship ever seen – and the biggest flop.

1859 – Charles Darwin gobsmacked all Christians by writing *The Origin of the Species* in which he stated that God had got it wrong and that we developed from monkeys. Further proof of this can be seen in the P.G. Tips ads.

1870 – Home Rule was a term created for the Irish demand for self-government.

1874 – Levi Strauss invented jeans in America, I wonder if he realised that it was to become THE uniform.

Chapter 37

Glad To Be Gladstone – 1865

Palmerston was dead and the two contenders for his job were Disraeli, the Conservative, and Gladstone, the Liberal. Disraeli kicked off, and in an attempt to woo the working class, passed another Reform Bill in 1867. The canny poor weren't having any of it, however. The following year they chucked him out in favour of Gladstone. This peeved Victoria because although she really liked Disraeli, she thought Gladstone a 'deluded old fanatic' (her words). She once commented, 'He speaks to me as if I were a public meeting,' which I think's quite funny for a queen.

Nevertheless, reforms followed thick and fast and were as follows:

1. Voting was made secret.
2. The army was reorganised so the rich and priviliged couldn't buy themselves commissions (to be officers).
3. Trade Unions were made legal (at long last).
4. A Land Act protected tenants from their unscrupulous landlords (at longer last).
5. The Anglican church chucked out of Ireland.
6. Universities were open to all (unless you were thick).
7. Primary schools were finally introduced in 1870 (but you didn't have to go).
8. Not really a reform I suppose. Victoria allowed the Anti-Homosexual Bill (poor Bill) to go through, but, as she couldn't even conceive that lesbianism was possible, struck out any female references.

Unfortunately, it was too much change too soon and poor old Gladstone had to swop with Disraeli again. Anyone for tennis?

1877 – Empress of India

Meanwhile, being just a queen was turning out to be a bit downmarket for Victoria. Disraeli, who was always looking for

different ways of being even more popular (creep), offered her the chance of being an Empress in 1877, which she jumped at. OK, it was only Empress of India, but you've got to start somewhere. Disraeli, now her favourite Prime Minister, took over a big chunk of South Africa in the famous 'Scramble for Africa', but Parliament changed ends again and spoilsport Gladstone gave it back to the Boers (Dutch farmers). Vicky even came out of retirement to join in the scrap.

1884 – The Irish Question

Everything came to a head over Home Rule for Ireland (so what's new?). The Liberals thought Ireland should mind its own business and the Conservatives thought we should mind it for them (in a nutshell). Gladstone's colleagues rebelled and the Liberals and Irish Nationalists were beat hands down. Gladstone resigned after fourteen years in office and the Irish question was left – all together now – unsettled.

1885 – Lord Salisbury

Disraeli was dead and Gladstone retired. Now we either had Lord Salisbury who, although a fine Conservative, is largely remembered for being the last Prime Minister to have a beard; or Lord Rosebery, who is largely remembered for being one of the first not to (no crummy Thatcher jokes please!).

Poor old Victoria was getting a touch ancient but Britain was strong, cocky and fighting fit. Apart from the Crimean War and that bit of trouble in India our Empire was behaving itself. Britain was becoming 'The workshop of the world' and 'abroad' was queuing up to buy whatever we made. London had by this time also become the world's financial centre.

1886 – Europe

By now, however, things were looking a bit different. America and the united countries of Europe (dominated by the horrible Hun), were catching up and nibbling at our heels. The thing that got the Europeans hot and bothered was that, unlike Great Britain, they didn't have any possessions abroad (to exploit) and they were dead jealous.

It was the Belgians (who are they? You might ask) who were sniffing around Africa and had already nabbed the Congo. We weren't doing too badly, having grabbed Nigeria, Kenya, Nyasaland (now Malawi) and Rhodesia (now Zambia and Zimbabwe) and sharing the Sudan with Egypt. Only the Germans who'd bagged Tanganyika (now Tanzania) prevented us from controlling everything from South Africa to Cairo.

1886 – Africa

When gold fever hit the Transvaal – a Dutch Republic which the Boers set up to get away from the British – it was invaded by British 'cowboys' determined to make a killing (financially). When, with inimitable British cheek, these invaders demanded the vote, a huge scrap broke out which quickly developed into the Boer War. The whole world thought we were creeps but in the end we won and the Transvaal and the Orange Free State became ours in 1902. And what creeps we were! The British burned most of the Boer farms and herded the occupants into 'concentration camps'. Thousands died in these atrocious places much to the horror of the British at home. It has been said that these camps gave Hitler (coming soon) his very worst ideas.

1888 – At Home

At home the Local Government Act replaced a system unchanged since Tudor times. Education was made free. Even though the

Factories Act and the Housing Act were passed, most of the working class were still appallingly poverty stricken. Trade Unionism was crouched ready to leap in and kick the exploiting employers where it hurt most. In 1893 Keir Hardie founded the first Independent Labour Party and in 1900 a conference of the Trade Unions, Socialist Societies, and the new Co-operative Movement, formed the Labour party that we know today. In the same year Gladstone tried to get Home Rule for Ireland again. It was okay with the Commons but the Lords would have none of it and kicked it out.

By this time the European situation was looking extremely poorly. The struggle to snatch colonies had led to a full-blown arms race. Europe was split into two huge camps with Germany, Austria and Italy on one side, and France and Russia on the other. Britain stayed 'Splendidly Aloof' but watched nervously as the Krauts built a fleet to shoo us off the waves (which Britannia ruled), and started supporting the boring Boers, who were getting a bit fed up with being bossed around by the British in Africa.

By the Way
In 1888 the world's best known murderer, Jack The Ripper, was roaming the streets of East London. He murdered ten prostitutes, with names like 'Clay Pipe Alice' and 'Carroty Nell', in such a horrible way that the police thought he must have been a surgeon. His identity is a mystery to this day. At least ten movies and 200 books have described his lurid exploits.

Meanwhile

1876 – Alexander Graham Bell rang someone on the phone he'd just invented (and probably got a wrong number).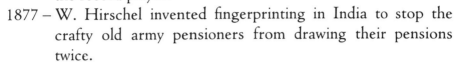

1877 – Thomas Edison invented the record player.

1877 – W. Hirschel invented fingerprinting in India to stop the crafty old army pensioners from drawing their pensions twice.

1878 – Cleopatra's Needle a 3,500-year-old priceless obelisk brought from Egypt in a specially designed ship called the *Cleopatra* (what a coincidence). It was erected on the Thames Embankment to commemorate our victory over Napoleon.

1885 – Karl Benz, a German, drove the first successful petrol-driven car (a Merc?).

1886 – Coca Cola is invented in America, and advertised as 'Esteemed Brain Tonic and Intellectual Beverage'. Bet they were glad when they thought of 'The Real Thing'.

1892 – Zip Fastener invented and called the C-Curity. Unfortunately, the inventor hadn't got it quite right and it was liable to spring open at any time (very embarrassing!).

1893 – First breakfast cereal, Shredded Wheat, invented by H K Perky (I bet he was).

1895 – First movie shown in Paris.

1895 – Marconi turned on the first wireless (and probably got the Archers).

1897 – Thomas Edison switched on the first light bulb.

Chapter 38

Eddie For King – 1901

When poor little old Victoria died it was her dear son Edward's turn. He was sixty years old and, unlike his mum, liked to be seen out and about having a good time. It's fair to say that the British had had enough of a ruler who was always behind closed curtains. I suppose if you're paying all that money, you want to see something for it.

The country, by this time, needed very little maintenance from the top as it was now totally run by Parliament. This left Edward with loads of free time to indulge his many pleasurable pastimes. He was always to be seen at the race tracks, at the theatre, and with women who definitely weren't his wife.

It's fair to say that he wasn't the cleverest king we've ever had, hating anything that required the slightest bit of concentration. He once described the first submarine, which he had to inspect, as 'very complicated, with lots of brass'. Sounds like a man after my own heart.

He had married a Danish princess called Alexandra in 1863 who was not only popular with the great British public, but also with her mother-in-law (the queen), who by that time was a grouchy old misery and not at all easy to please. Edward's favourite pastime was one of the worst kept secrets in history and his lady 'friends' included Jennie Churchill (Winston's mum) and Lillie Langtry (the famous actress).

Edward VII and the French

Don't get the impression, however, that Edward was a useless king. As a diplomat he really did the business, especially over in France, where he was often to be seen – usually in Paris – usually having a 'bon' time – and usually with someone he shouldn't have been with. This popularity with the French (highly suspicious?) led to the Treaty of Alliance called the Entente Cordiale in 1904 which was to become 'trés' useful as you will soon see.

Edward's loose lifestyle caught up with him, and he was only to reign for nine years, dying in 1910.

By the Way

The Labour Party first appeared in Parliament in 1906 when twenty-nine MPs were returned. There were already twenty-two Trade Unionist MPs who, although attached to the Liberals, were really more inclined to Labour.

Meanwhile

1901 – Rudyard Kipling wrote the *Just So Stories*.
1903 – First aeroplane flight by the Wright brothers in America.
1905 – Hubert Booth invented the first vacuum cleaner (horse-drawn). When first used in London it was so noisy it caused the horses to bolt (with the vacuum cleaner!).

1909 – Henry Ford manufactured the first production line car – the Model T. You could have any colour, he said, as long as it was black!

1909 – Bleriot managed to fly the English Channel.

1910 – Huge balloons called Zeppelins used as the first commercial air service and later to bomb London. Why didn't we pop them?

1911 – Ernest Rutherford found a proton (a who – ton?).

1912 – *Titanic* hit an iceberg and 1513 poor passengers drowned.

1912 – George Bernard Shaw wrote *Pygmalion*, a story about a common young miss what gets posh.

1913 – Stravinsky's *Rite of Spring* booed off stage in London.

1914 – Ernest Swinton invented the tank for Britain (came in useful).

1917 – The Russian Revolution. Tsar Nicholas abdicates. Lenin and the Bolsheviks take power. Royalty went out – Communism came in.

Chapter 39:

War Of The World

At the time of Victoria's death the Prime Minister was Balfour, a Conservative, but by 1906 the Liberals had swept him away.

They had promised the grumbling workers they'd put a stop to the rising prices and falling wages. Campbell-Bannerman, and later Lord Asquith, went a long way to achieving this and also brought in free grub for school children; slum clearance; and fixed minimum wages (they were ridiculously low, but at least fixed). You don't get anything for nothing in this life, and cash had to be found to pay for the many reforms. They looked, for the first time, towards the rich landowners and decided to tax them properly – and about time too.

When Lloyd George (who looked a bit like Charlie Chaplin) proposed a further super tax, swiftly followed by – shock – horror – a land tax, the House of Lords boiled over and squealed like stuck piglets. They rejected the whole new budget, and most of the reforms for good measure.

1910 – George V

By this time we had a new king (George V), who seemed quite a reasonable bloke. Lloyd George appealed to him to help squash the power of the loaded Lords. This, surprisingly, he did and the Lords, even more surprisingly, put their aristocratic hands up and gave in. From then on, the House of Lords has only been somewhere warm to go for a few doddery old ex-politicians and the rather inbred relics of our nobility's glorious past. The House of Commons, from that point in history, called all the shots as Britain's sole legislative body.

1911 – Politicians

In 1911 MPs started to be paid. In the past, all politicians were either self-made men, or had come from old money. Either way, they were definitely not short of a few quid. By giving them a salary of £450 a year (now £20,000) it meant, at last, that ordinary working chaps could (if voted for) get a seat in the Commons. The Trade Unions were also allowed to shove cash in their candidates' back pockets – a decision which was to change British politics to this day.

When the reforms came, however, it was a bit like locking the stable door after the horse had bolted. Britain was in the full flow of social turmoil or, in other words, fed up to the back teeth. There were serious strikes, particularly of the miners and railwaymen; the Suffragettes started chaining themselves to railings as a protest, fed

up with waiting for the women's vote; Welsh non-conformists were baying for the dis-establishment of their Church, and the Irish Nationalists were demanding Home Rule yet again. By 1914 the southern Catholics were on the verge of civil war with the Protestant Orangemen of Ulster (the same old problem).

When the natives become restless, there's nothing like a Royal wedding or a war to unite them. As Britain's royalty had no one to marry off, it seemed like the trouble brewing in Europe could be rather timely.

1914 – Trouble with Germany Again

Germany was still up to its old tricks, trying to expand its Empire by bullying defenceless little countries; and Austria had upset the Russians by snatching Bosnia and Herzegovina. The arms race changed gear and in 1914 when a silly Serb murdered the heir to the Austrian Empire the powder keg finally blew.

Austria declared war on Serbia – Germany on Russia and France. When the Krauts invaded Belgium (which Lloyd George called a 'little five-foot five nation'), Britain drew its guns and declared war as it had done years before when France and Spain had tried the same thing.

Britain's Allies

If it seems a bit like David challenging Goliath, it wasn't. Luckily we had some big tough boys to stand behind us. Canada, Australia, New Zealand, South Africa, and even India and Ireland, were in our gang and prepared to roll their sleeves up and get stuck in. Mind you, having said all that, they didn't have much choice did they?

Soon the whole world was tearing itself apart and, by the time the Yanks joined the fray in 1917, Britain alone had lost 1,000,000

of its young men, mostly in the disgusting trench warfare of France.

Before long, however, Germany was on its knees. By 1918 they'd lost the war, all their colonial empire, a big bit of their European territory, all their fleet and all their money – and it jolly well served them right. But did it teach them a lesson? Wait and see.

1918 – League of Nations

Something worthwhile did seem to come from the Great War. President Wilson of the United States suggested an international association to prevent the same thing happening again (oh dear! oh dear!). Everyone promised to behave themselves except Russia and – can you believe it – the United States, who said it was too idealistic.

Wars are funny things. Apart from reducing the population in a rather dramatic way, they sometimes have surprising side effects. The British had become united against the common foe; the class system and the battles between the workers and their bosses being

143

almost forgotten. The Suffragettes got the vote for all women – as a prize for being so helpful in the war. After the First World War business boomed for a couple of years and everything looked OK for a prosperous future, so we didn't have to have a Royal wedding!

1919 – Ireland Again

Things weren't so rosy in Ireland – surprise! surprise! Not only were they after Home Rule, but now the extremist Sinn Feiners wanted a totally independent Republic. The long expected civil war broke out, at last, and Parliament sent thousands of out of work ex-soldiers (called the Black and Tans) to sort them out. A good comparison could be made between their nickname and the Rottweiler dog's colouring. They were just as vicious and brainless, making things much, much worse.

Finally, to cut a long war short, Ireland was split in two. The southern Irish Free State in the south, and the rest in the north.

If only they'd thought of this in Tudor times, centuries of violent, Irish, argy-bargy might have been saved (or might not!).

The Depression

The post-war boom was short lived and the 20s and 30s brought a terrible slump. Anyone who did manage to make anything couldn't sell it as most of the 'civilised' world was flat broke. Even America was depressed (poor thing), and as for central Europe, it was on the verge of starvation (wars are jolly fun, aren't they?).

Britain was one of the last to fall, but when it did, it really scraped the bottom of the barrel. Hunger marches and strikes followed huge unemployment. Surprisingly, the figure of 3,000,000 out of work was about the same as it is now (OK I know the population was smaller!).

Labour, as always in hard times, gained more and more support, becoming the third great political party. In 1922 the Conservatives didn't want to play any more and left Lloyd George's coalition. Unfortunately, they took the ball with them, and Bonar Law (daftest name for a PM yet), followed shortly by Stanley Baldwin (who sounds like a northern footballer), formed a Conservative government. They prescribed protectionism as the sweet pill that would make everything better. It didn't, and soon, inevitably, the first Labour government, headed by Ramsay MacDonald, knocked them out, offering a different-flavoured pill to make everything better. It didn't work either, and Stan Baldwin came back with a vast majority. What happened to the Liberals? Don't ask! From that day on, Lloyd George, and the Liberals, were never to be a serious threat to the Conservatives or Labour again.

1924 – Winston Churchill

Baldwin's chancellor was Winston Churchill, who re-imposed import duties to protect ourselves from cheapo imports. Unfortunately, by returning to the gold standard (please don't ask), he made our products more expensive which made the depression even worse. By 1926 the cat was completely out of the bag and a General Strike hit Britain like a sledgehammer. It only lasted ten days and then collapsed taking the Trade Union Council with it. Acts were swiftly passed to keep these naughty unions in order, but this upset the workers so much that they voted Labour again, welcoming MacDonald back in 1929.

Then – shock, horror! – the American economy hit the deck, and the rest of the world's economy slipped further down the cliff. Old MacDonald formed a 'National Government'. This is a clever political trick that a not-very-good government uses when it hasn't got a blinking clue how to get itself out of the sh . . . ambles. It really means that by sharing the power with the other party you don't cop all the blame yourself. The joke was that this Parliament had 471 Conservatives but only 52 Labour members, so poor old Mac was left leading practically an all-Conservative government which was a bit embarrassing.

C'MON YOU KRAUTS!

Meanwhile

1919 – Alcock and Brown managed to fly the Atlantic.

1922 – Broadcasting started from the BBC.

1926 – Baird invented something called a television.

1927 – Charles Lindbergh ran out of pals so flew the Atlantic alone.

1927 – First talking pictures. Cinema owners finally shot the piano players.

1928 – The great Walt Disney gave birth to the even greater Mickey Mouse.

1929 – US stock market collapsed heralding another world depression.

1930 – The first supermarket opened in New York.

Chapter 40:

Back At The Palace – 1936

When George V died his eldest boy Edward VIII was next in line and the British Empire, now called the Commonwealth, were delighted as he'd spent so much time visiting them. All except India who were fed up with the British and wanted them to clear out. Unfortunately, Edward had this American girlfriend called Mrs

Simpson, who was not only still married, but had been married before (tut! tut!). This went down like a lead balloon with the government, who told him it was to be her or the crown. Apparently it's just not done to have divorced AMERICAN women as queens. (I'd have thought anything was better than Germans.) Anyway, they obviously thought it was a flash in the pan and that he'd give her up. They were wrong for only ten months later he threw in the sponge and told the country they could have their goddam crown back.

1936 – George VI
Edward's younger brother Bertie (Albert), was a bit surprised to get a new job (King), and a new name (George). He did, however, have a nice wife (the now Queen Mother) and two little girls (our Queen and Princess Margaret) and was generally thought to be far more suitable than his naughty brother. Just to show no hard feelings he gave his poor elder brother the title HRH Duke of Windsor; and Mrs Simpson (when she'd got shot of Mr Simpson) became an all-American English Duchess. Her mother-in-law, however, the old Queen Mary, wouldn't have her in the house and was never to speak to her (that's mothers-in-law for you).

By the Way
During the period of poor Edward's abdication in 1936, he hit the brandy and soda so heavily that he had to have his stomach pumped.

Chapter 41:

Bad To Worse

If you think Britain had been through some hard times, hold on to your seats. While we'd been absorbed in a General Strike, hunger marches and miscellaneous mayhem, Japan invaded Manchuria. The League of Nations wagged its corporate finger and told the pesky little Japs to behave. Japan promptly said 'shan't', and refused to play any more, promptly pulling out, followed shortly by Germany in 1933.

At this time news was coming from Germany of a funny little painter and decorator with a strange haircut and a daft moustache, who was promising his fellow countrymen a way out of the appalling economic mess they were in. His name was Adolf Hitler, and he was to win the 'World Bad Guy Record' of all time. His nationalism knew no bounds, and the National Socialist Party swept through the German nation like Beatlemania through Britain in the sixties. The Nazis, as they soon became known, hated anything remotely foreign, making the tall, blue-eyed, blond-haired caricature German a standard which they all had to aspire to. Strangely enough, Hitler himself was short and dark but no one dared mention that.

1935 – Hitler and Fascism
What his 'Brown Shirts', and later his Secret Service, did to the gypsies and Jews has no place in a 'funny' book, but one can say

that, years after, the rest of the world finds it very difficult to trust Germany again. Mind you, it would be untruthful to pretend that there wasn't fascism in Britain. In fact, a nasty bit of work called Sir Oswald Mosley spearheaded the anti-Jewish movement. He bought a load of black shirts for his fascist mates and tried to stir this hatred up in England, only to be arrested and thrown into jail.

By this time you had to be blind or stupid not to see the potential 'aggro' in Europe. Hitler occupied the Rhineland, and the Spanish Civil War had broken out between the idealistic Communists and the Fascists. Japan then declared war on China. Italy, probably realising it was going to join the baddies' side, pulled out of the League of Nations, leaving it like a toothless lion.

Hitler now really had the bit between his teeth and took on almost Godlike status with the sheeplike Krauts. He incorporated Austria with Germany and conquered Czechoslovakia. Mussolini (him of the silly pointy hat) led Italy to crush Albania and waited eagerly to see if Hitler would smash Poland (it sounds a bit like the World Cup!).

1939 – Chamberlain Asks Nicely

France and Britain promised Poland that they wouldn't let those nasty Germans get away with it. Neville Chamberlain, our new Conservative PM, went over to Germany to ask Herr Hitler, nicely, to promise to be a good fascist and leave Poland alone. He came back wreathed in smiles saying that Hitler wasn't really a bad bloke and that everything would be all right. Hitler obviously thought he was a right wally and on September 1st 1939 he invaded Poland, sticking two fingers in the air at Britain and France (remember? Go forth and multiply). This was the last straw and on the 3rd, we both declared war on Germany and the fight really started.

Chapter 42

World War II

THE SIDES

The Allies	Axis Countries
Great Britain	(the Enemy)
France	Germany
Russia	Italy
South Africa	Japan
Australia	
New Zealand	
Canada	
America	

It seems rather unbalanced when looked at this way, but at the very beginning of the war it was very different. If you are wondering what happened to all the other countries, they were mostly overrun by the Germans or the Japanese very quickly.

1939 – Bleak Prospects

Things started badly and by 1940 the Krauts had ousted British troops from France who quickly surrendered. Nevertheless the Brits were united as never before, largely due to Churchill's rousing oratory – 'Never have so few owed so much to so many' – or words

OLIVER CHURCHILL   WINSTON HARDY

Spot the Difference.

to that effect. It didn't take long before everyone had taken sides and the fighting had spread all over the world. Hitler had conquered most of Europe and was concentrating on Egypt and the western Deserts. At first our 'Desert Rats' really showed the Italians how to fight in these dreadful conditions but when Rommel and the infamous German Afrika Korps turned up it was a different story and we really had the sand kicked in our faces. It was a combination of our brilliant little General Montgomery and the arrival (just in time) of the Americans in their fab Sherman tanks that eventually caused the Germans to surrender their buckets and spades and leave the beach. Gradually the allies started getting the upper hand and when Hitler tried to invade Russia in 1941, the 'Great Bear' shook itself and joined in the fray.

1941 – America Joins In

One of the great turning points had been when the Japs attacked and destroyed a large part of the American fleet at Pearl Harbour. This had really caused the Yanks to explode and their mighty army, who'd been standing by, sprang into action. Suddenly everything looked very different. Italy finally surrendered in 1943 having not really had a very good war.

By the way, here's an old wartime joke:– What's the shortest book in the world? Answer: The book of Italian war heroes!

Meanwhile at home the British were having the fight of their lives:

The Royal Air Force

On our side we had the amazing little Spitfires and Hurricanes, but they were greatly outnumbered by the Messerschmitts and Stukas of the mighty German air force which was called the Luftwaffe.

The air battles that took place over England supplied the British film industry with material that was to keep it busy for the next thirty years. Our boys were always portrayed as brave, good looking, clean shaven, Biggles types who were kind to their wives, children and pets.

The filthy German pilots, on the other hand, had mean, unshaven faces and were always played by the same brutish actors who, had we ever followed them home, would have cheated on zeir Frauleins and vipped zeir Dachshunds.

The Royal Navy

The same was true at sea. Our officers were all shown as pipe smoking, duffel coated, frightfully upper class Nigel Havers types. Below decks the lower ranks were quaint, honest cockneys, who knew their place and when shot or drowned, died quietly (clutching pictures of their mums), without complaining.

The horrible Hun, on the other side, skulked around in their U-boats, sneaking up behind our brave lads and shooting them in the backs (typical). When they were sinking (which was pretty regular), the Germans made dreadful fusses, shouting and scream-ing like nobody's business, and cursing the far-too-clever British navy (three cheers!).

These were the films, however, and it must be said that, though their cause was rotten, many of the Germans were astounding soldiers.

Invasion?

Again the war had come just in time to help the British populace forget how much they hated each other. At one stage it looked very likely that we might be invaded for the first time since William the Conqueror in 1066. (Hitler the Conqueror?)

It was just as well the German stormtroopers didn't get to Britain, as all we had to stop them was our funny little Home Guard. These were volunteer 'soldiers', usually of advanced years, whose job was to protect our women, children and pets with not much more than garden tools.

Advance at your Peril!

Chapter 43:

England Digs In

When it looked as if the German invasion was imminent, the bombing raids became as regular as milk deliveries, and the British put up a fight the like of which had never been seen before or since. Huge, Zeppelin-like balloons hung over major cities, not to tell where the party was, but to make sure the attacking planes couldn't fly too low. Most city families dug shelters in their back yards. Those that didn't have back yards, dived into communal shelters as soon as they heard the air raid sirens. These dreadful sirens made such a horrid eery din, that they were almost as frightening as the raids themselves.

In central London, which obviously caught the brunt of Germany's fury, everyone hurried into the Underground for late night protection. Funny really – nowadays protection is the last thing you'd get! City children were evacuated to stay with their country cousins, but they were often like oil and water – the streetwise city kids finding country life difficult to cope with. This, combined with terrible homesickness, caused many to drift back to their families before the end of the war. Food, clothes and petrol were rationed and luxuries like fruit, chocolate and nylon stockings were not to be seen again for years, apart from those given as presents by the American soldiers when they eventually arrived.

They gave their chewing gum, cigarettes and stockings, from their military bases, to all our best-looking girls (while our boys were away).

Our new Royal couple, George and Elizabeth, proved a great boost to the morale of the British people. They spent much of their time in the centre of London, regularly visiting the homeless and injured, even though their own home (Buck House) was hit nine times.

1940 – The Bombing
Thousands of homes, and the people in them, were destroyed by the appalling night bombing raids, but the British refused to give in. Never in our history did we think the suffering so justified or the enemy so revolting.

Towards the end of the war the ghastly Germans developed the nastiest weapon that had ever been seen – or not seen! It was a petrol-driven guided missile called a V1 (later the V2), launched from somewhere in Holland. They were the first totally unmanned attack vehicles and were nicknamed 'Doodlebugs'. Everyone was terrified of them as, although they could be heard approaching, at the last minute the engines would cut out. It was anybody's guess where (and on who) they might land.

1944 – The Grand Finale

France was liberated in 1944, Hitler then kindly killed himself (about time too!) and in 1945 Germany gave in. They had lost 4½ million people and most of their cities were destroyed. America, just to make sure, dropped the biggest bomb ever seen on Hiroshima and the Japanese put their hands up.

The war was over. The horrible Hun was beat. Good had triumphed over evil – and Britain could now get back to its internal (and eternal) feuding again.

Bibliography

C.W. Airne, *The Story of Prehistoric and Roman Britain,* Thomas Hope & Sankey-Hudson Ltd.

Guy Arnold, *Book of Dates: A Chronology of World History,* Kingfisher/Grisewood & Dempsey, 1983

Roy Burrell, *The Oxford Children's History, Vol I,* Oxford University Press, 1983

F.E. Halliday, *A Concise History of England,* Thames & Hudson, 1964

J.A. Hammerton (ed.), *Harmsworth's Universal Encyclopedia,* The Amalgamated Press Ltd.

M.C. Scott Moncrieff, *Kings and Queens of England,* Blandford Press, 1966

Kenneth O. Morgan (ed.), *Oxford Illustrated History of Britain,* Oxford University Press, 1984

Odhams Press, *The British Encyclopedia,* 1933

Peter & Mary Speed, *The Oxford Children's History Vol. II,* Oxford University Press, 1983

The Reader's Digest Assoc. Ltd., *The Last Two Million Years,* 1973

The Reader's Digest Assoc. Ltd., *Strange Series/Amazing Facts,* 1975

R.J. Unstead, *Looking At History,* A & C Black Ltd., 1955

David Walleninsky, Irving Wallace, Amy Wallace, Sylvia Wallace, *The Book of Lists, Vol. I,* 1977. *Vol. II,* 1980